NICE

WEEKEND**escape**

Venice:
city of canals

Venice, a city famous for its waterways, has been charming people since the Middle Ages, and has no intention of changing. Like the endless succession of writers, painters, musicians and film-makers who have come here, and the many thousands of visitors who are stunned by Venice's beauty each year, you too will undoubtedly fall under its magical spell.

As you explore Venice, the palaces of the Grand Canal, St Mark's Square with its pigeons, and the gondolas gliding silently across the lagoon all help bring this magical city to life. The churches and museums, the festivals that have been celebrated for decades, the sumptuous cafés with their sunlit terraces, the famous jewelers and the luxury fabric and antique shops will all charm you. And when you wander along its winding alleyways, Venice

Goldoni; to listen to the music of Vivaldi beneath the vaults of a Gothic church or a palace; to drift along in a gondola on the illuminated Grand Canal or to go for a drink in one of the city's many bars – it's up to you. All you have to do is choose between the city's many attractions. But be warned – it won't be easy!

However you decide to spend your time, you'll find the weekend will simply fly by. And be warned, once you've fallen under its spell, Venice will draw you back time and time again.

will reveal itself to be so much more than just a museum city or tempting shopping center. It will surprise you by revealing its other face, that of a city with charming hidden residential districts. As you stroll through the city, you may find yourself walking alongside a quiet *rio* (river), where truck farmers' boats overflowing with fruit and vegetables are moored, before emerging into a little *campo* (square) full of children playing.

The next minute, you may have to elbow your way through a narrow *calle* (street). Carried along by the crowd, you may sometimes find it difficult to stop to look in the tempting shop-windows filled with Murano glass or Burano lace, the *legatorie* (stationery stores) with their unique marbled paper, the grocery stores with their displays of rainbow-colored pasta, or the mask shops where skilled craftsmen create fantastic and colorful works of art using leather or papier-mâché.

In the evening, after a memorable dinner at a little *osteria*, you'll find plenty of other pleasures in store for you. You may decide to go to a theater, where you'll be delighted by the works of

How to get there

By plane

From the UK
Easyjet (☎ 0870 6 000 000 www.easyjet.com) and **British Airways** (☎ 0870 850 9850 www.britishairways.com) both fly direct to Venice.
Ryan Air (☎ 0871 246 0000 www.ryanair.com) flies to Treviso Airport, which is a short train or bus ride from the center of city.

From the US and other departure points

There are no direct flights from the United States, Canada, Australia or New Zealand. However, the following major airlines can arrange your connection to Venice with a code share or another airline from major European hubs, usually London or Rome.

Alitalia
www.alitalia.com
This website is packed with flight information and includes contact details for their offices worldwide.

American Airlines
www.americanairlines.com
Flies to Rome via London, Brussels or Zurich.

Air Canada
www.aircanada.ca
Flies to Rome via Frankfurt or London.

Cathay Pacific
www.cathaypacific.com
Fly daily from Sydney and Melbourne via Hong Kong.

Arriving at the airport

The Marco Polo airport is about 12 km (7.5 miles) from Venice, north-east of the town. ATMs are located in the departure terminal. If you need fresh cash when you arrive, take the escalator to get to the *partenze* (departures) terminal. To get to San Marco, you have several alternatives:

– No. 5 bus (ACTV) will take you to the Piazzale Roma in 20 mins. Two departures per hour (at 10 after and 20 to the hour). Allow €2, more if you have a lot of luggage.

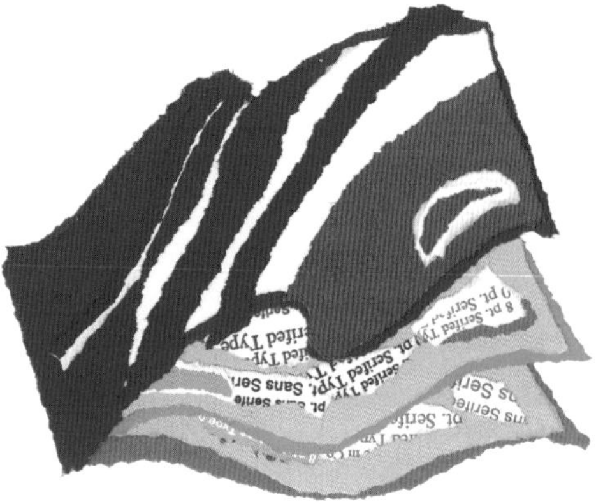

– the ATVO bus is the same as bus no. 5. Two departures per hour (at 10 after and 20 to the hour). Allow €3, luggage included.

Once you've arrived at the Piazzale Roma terminal, take the *vaporetto* (water bus) to get to your hotel or, like hundreds of people every day, walk there. A suitcase on wheels is ideal.

– Alilaguna boats link the airport, Fondamente Nove, Murano, Lido, San Marco and Zattere. You can estimate 1h and €10 to reach San Marco. Departures every hour. Information and timetable on www.alilaguna.it.

To get from the airport to the landing stage, allow a good five minutes on foot. There is also a free shuttle.

You can obtain your tickets from the desks at the arrival terminal (left as you come out of customs). Alternatively, you can buy it on board the Alilaguna. More information: ☎ 041 260 92 40, www.veniceairport.it or www.hellovenezia.it

– Finally, the lovely *taxi acquei* (water taxis) are another means of getting to Venice, certainly the quickest one. For example, the trip from the airport to the Accademia Bridge costs around €80 for 2 people. In fact, more often than not €100.

PREPARING YOUR WEEKEND ON THE NET

www.gazzettino.it: site about daily life in the north-west of Italy. Click on the Venezia tab and you will get the latest news in Italian.

www.hellovenezia.it and **www.turismovenezia.it** are two sites giving general tourist information.

www.culturaspettacolovenezia.it and **www.veneziacultura.it** are more specifically geared to information about cultural events.

www.unospitedivenezia.it and **www.veneziadavivere.com** are full of practical information, including concert dates and the latest places to go out. Read the section "Practical Information" in the Going Out section (p. 128).

AVERAGE TEMPERATURES IN °C/°F

	Minimum	Maximum
Jan.-Mar.	1-5/34-41	6-12/43-54
Apr.-Jun	10-18/50-64	17-25/63-77
Jul.-Sep.	20-17/68-83	28-25/82-77
Oct.-Dec.	11-2/52-36	12-8/54-46

By train

Eurostar/SNCF

Information and reservations:
www.eurostar.com
www.voyages-sncf.com
It is possible to catch a train directly to Venice from Paris, itself not much more than 2 hours from London by Eurostar. Daily departure from Paris Bercy at 8.28pm, arriving in Venice at 8.55am.
From €35 per person for a one-way ticket in a 6-berth car; from €60 in a 4-berth carriage; and from €120 in a Double Cabin. Reservations available 90 days before departure date.

Venice Simplon Orient-Express

Information and reservations:
☎ 0845 077 2222 (UK);
☎ 1 866 674 3689 (US/Can)
www.orient-express.com
This luxurious train dating back to a bygone era links Paris (from the Gare de l'Est) to Venice in about 20 hours (departure around 9.40pm arrival around 5.30pm). A refined cuisine is served on board. The Venice Simplon runs from March to November from Thursdays through Sundays. Allow €1,785 per person for a one-way ticket. Specialist tour operators can arrange connections from London or other European cities.

Arriving by train

It is a great moment! The Venezia-Santa Lucia station (do not get off at the Venezia Mestre station) is located along the Grand Canal. From Ferrovia station, *vaporetti* numbers 1 and 82 will take you to the Piazza San Marco (ticket €5).

Packages and tour operators

Travel agents and "no frills stays" on the Internet offer weekend packages for 2, 3 or 4 days including flight (or train ride) and hotel, from 2 to 4 stars. Your travel agent will advise you about the best deals. There is a definite advantage: You don't have to worry about reservations and the agency's special rates are always cheaper than the prices offered to the general public. Why not use this opportunity to stay in a luxury hotel at a reduced

ITALIAN STATE TOURIST OFFICES (ENIT)

US
630 Fifth Avenue
Suite 1565
New York
☎ 212 245 4822
www.italiantourism.com

UK
1 Princes Street
London W1R 8AY
☎ 020 7408 1254
www.italiantouristboard.co.uk

cost? If you opt for a package, watch out for the time of flights: A very late departure and very early return can severely shorten a weekend. Other packages automatically include the Saturday night in a hotel there. Finally, in Venice, avoid choosing a hotel on the Lido: You would waste time with transportation. For a two to three days' stay that is important, unless the price is particularly advantageous.

Renting a car

To rent a car, go to the usual agencies at the airport: Avis, ☎ 041 541 50 30; Hertz, ☎ 041 541 61 51; Italy by Car, ☎ 041 541 60 49).

When to go

In winter, the Adriatic coast is often cold and windswept. In addition to the Bora, freezing cold air accompanied by a few snowflakes sometimes blows down from the neighboring Alps. If you time your visit to coincide with the Carnival, remember to take some warm clothes, including a coat, gloves and raincoat. It can rain in Venice until the end of spring and an *acqua alta* can happen at any time in winter. The waters of the lagoon rise and flood the city center, making it impossible to get around (see p. 85).

The best time of year to visit is from late April to early July, when visitors really start to arrive in droves. In the late spring it rains less often, the air is mild and the long days allow you to dine out of doors in the light of the setting sun. Summer isn't necessarily such a good time of year to visit Venice. Apart from the crowds of tourists, the air can be unpleasantly humid. Clouds of insects, including mosquitoes (*zanzare*), sometimes take advantage of the climate to invade the lagoon and the water can smell very unpleasant. The fall, from September to November, is another good season to plan your visit. The days are shorter but the light is quite beautiful. The islands of the lagoon are sometimes noisy with migrating birds stopping off on their way to warmer climes. The weather is still fine and although there can be showers, they often don't last long. However, the nights are quite cool from September onward. Think about taking some warm layers and possibly an insect repellent against mosquitoes. Your choice of season may, of course, depend on the large number of festivals and other events taking place in the city.

VENICE IN LITERATURE

The Merchant of Venice, by William Shakespeare; *Portraits of Places by* Henry James; *Death in Venice,* by Thomas Mann; *Innocents Abroad* by Mark Twain; *The Story of My Life* by Giacomo Casanova; *Don't Look Now* by Daphne du Maurier (made into a movie in the 1970's with Donald Sutherland and Julie Christie); *Venice: Tales of the City,* a collection of different writers' impressions of Venice. Venice also appears in the literature of other famous authors including Hemingway, Goethe, Proust, Byron and Sollers.

Insurance

If you pay for your ticket by credit card, you automatically benefit from some insurance regarding your luggage, the possible cancellation of your trip and medical repatriation. Find out more from your credit card company or ask your bank. EU citizens can also reclaim potential health costs once back in the UK; make sure you take an EHIC with you (available from post offices). Non-EU citizens should make sure they have adequate cover. The cost is low but it offers real benefits in case of problems.

Entry requirements and time

EU citizens should carry a valid ID card or passport. Non-EU citizens will require a valid passport, although US citizens do not require a visa to enter Italy. No vaccinations are required. Venice summer time is 2 hours ahead of GMT; winter time is GMT + 1 hour.

Customs

For travelers returning to other EU countries, there are few restrictions on alcohol or tobacco products. The only stipulation is that the goods must be for personal use and guidelines are provided, for example 10 liters of spirits, 90 liters of wine and 800 cigarettes. Duty-free limits for travelers leaving the EU are as follows:
Alcohol over 22%: 1L *or*
Alcohol not over 22%: 2L *and*
Still table wine: 2L
Cigarettes: 200 *or* cigars: 50 *or* tobacco 250gm
Perfume: 60ml
Toilet water: 250ml

Budget

Venice is a very expensive town, and this cannot be repeated often enough. With the *vaporetto* (€3.5 per trip, €5 for the Grand Canal), the entrance fees for churches (€2–€4), the museums (€6–€11), the glaring absence of printed guides in favor of paying audio guides, the cost of eating out (€25–€40), the hotel (between €100 and €150 a night on average for a double room), cappuccinos (€2–€6) and small glasses of white wine (€2–€3), you will easily go over budget even if the

smiles and kindness of the Venetians soften the pill.
In Venice, tourism is a flourishing industry and only Venetians themselves pay the real price, which you are better off not knowing! However, ice creams and cigarettes are cheap and the cost of dinner in a *bacaro* or a small *osteria* remains affordable. It is worth noting that picnics are not allowed in the city. Finally, be aware that buying an English book in Venice can cost you twice as much as at home.

Withdrawing money

Payment by credit card is not as widespread as in the UK or the US (except in the luxury boutiques in Venice).
Therefore, it is advisable to carry cash with you to pay for the restaurant check for example or for small souvenirs. You won't have any problems withdrawing money, whatever card you may be using: Ask a Venetian or someone at your hotel reception desk where the nearest ATM is. Otherwise, head for the Mercerie, the Strada Nuova, Campo Santa Marguerita, Accademia, calle larga XXII Marzo. Cash withdrawals from ATMs are usually subject to a bank commission: Ask your bank or download their charges before you go.
Banks are generally open every day, except for Saturdays and Sundays, from 8.30am to 1.30pm and from 3.30pm to 5pm.
Since January 1, 2002, the euro has replaced the old Italian currency, the lira, as it has most other currencies of the EU.

In case of loss or theft...

Venice is not a dangerous city, apart from the usual pickpockets in the most touristy areas. If you lose your credit card or have it stolen, contact the number provided by your bank or ask at the hotel reception desk. Before you leave home, make sure you photocopy both sides of your credit card and write down the address, phone number and fax of your bank. This will facilitate any procedures in case of loss or theft. Be careful and do the same with your passport and plane or train tickets.
Report any losses to the police. Many insurance companies require a police report to be submitted with a claim. The main police station has a special department to deal with visitors' problems:
via San Nicoladi 22
☎ 041 271 55 11

THE CATS OF VENICE

Venice couldn't have survived without its cats. Custodians of provisions and manuscripts, "cleaners" on ships (whether in the harbor or at sea, cats used to be taken on board), hunters on the canals, cats have always been held in high respect by Venetians. No rats, no plague.
During the Inquisition, as repression sounded the death knell for cats (Lucifer's creatures!) and rats reappeared with a vengeance, Venice was quick to start importing cats from the East again.
Today, their lagoon-green eyes are the result of a cross with these migrants. There are 12,000 felines to 80,000 Venetians, and an ongoing attachment between the two. As not all of the cats have owners, a charity, Dingo, feeds them and has them adopted and looked after.

Architecture and art

Since the Middle Ages, Venice, the Serenissima, has never ceased to fascinate the ambassadors, kings and travelers who came to visit. Every conceivable art form – gilded mosaics, countless pictures, numerous painted ceilings, grandiose sculpture and architecture, musicians, too – has enhanced the splendor of this very unusual city.

From Byzantine gold to Gothic elegance

It was only natural for Venice, a former colony of Constantinople, to turn first to Byzantine art. But it put its own particular stamp on it, expressing a need for its own brand of elegance. In the 11th century, for example, a Romanesque-influenced apse was grafted onto the Basilica di San Marco. The same thing happened the following century at S. S. Maria e Donato, which is reflected in the water of the Canal Grande of Murano. Enriched by trade with the Orient, Venice only adopted the Gothic style in the late 14th century. The architects of the Doges' Palace designed the heavy mass of the second floor to be supported by stone tracery, and had no hesitation in reversing the traditional laws of architecture. In palaces and churches elsewhere, builders favored slender lines and florid decoration.

Venice and the Renaissance

The Renaissance only came into its own on the lagoon in the 16th century. The architect Sansovino (1470–1529), who designed the loggia of the campanile of the Basilica San Marco, and above all Andrea Palladio (1508–1580), who was responsible for the geometrical forms of the Redentore on the Giudecca and San Giorgio Maggiore, are the two best representatives of the movement. It was at this time that Venetian painting produced its most talented artists. Giovanni Bellini (*c.*1430–1516), the inventor of the golden light that distantly recalls the mosaics of San Marco, trained the subtle artist Giorgione (*c.*1477–1510) and the "king of painters," Titian (*c.*1488–1576). Vittore Carpaccio (1455–1526) immortalized the Venetian festivals, while Tintoretto (1518–1594) and Veronese

Palazzo Labia in Venice.

(1528–1588) carried on the theatrical, and specifically Venetian, tradition.

The Baroque period and the Enlightenment

In the 17th century, Venice was the victim of repeated plague epidemics and economic crises. Artistic production suffered as a result, but nevertheless continued until the late 18th century and included such famous names as the architect Baldassare Longhena (1598–1682), who designed Santa Maria della Salute, and the playwright Carlo Goldoni (1707–1793), who wrote around a hundred comedies. Painting flourished: To the work of landscape artists such as Antonio Canaletto (1697–1768) and Francesco Gaudi (1712–1792), who portrayed the Serenissima in all its forms, was added the genre painting of Pietro Longhi (1702–1785) and the marvelous talent of Gianbattista Tiepolo (1696–1770). With these artists the Venetian school ended in a grand display of trompe l'œil and color.

VENICE, THE CRADLE OF OPERA

In 1637, a troupe of strolling players first performed an opera in a public theater in Venice. This experiment was such a success that theaters sprang up everywhere and an art form developed through which Venice could express its love of stage sets and machinery, in other words its need for show. Every period since has given rise to masterpieces that have exerted a considerable influence on European opera as a whole, including the operas of Monteverdi (1567–1643), Cavalli (1602–1676), Vivaldi (1678–1741) and the master of bel canto, Rossini (1792–1868).

Palaces
reflected in water

Starting with a number of handicaps, such as the absence of streets, the predominance of water and the palaces' dual role as stores and residences, the Venetian architects erected monuments that suited both changing fashions and their heritage. Their common efforts over the centuries have made the Grand Canal the most beautiful "street" in the world.

The Byzantine influence

The oldest palaces in Venice date from the 13th century and bear the mark of Byzantine influence. Their façades are recognizable by the arcaded portico covering practically the whole of the first floor (merchandise was unloaded here), as at the Fondaco dei Turchi, on the banks of the Grand Canal. Decoration remained discreet and for defensive reasons there were few openings in the walls of the palaces.

The Gothic taste

Times had changed, and Venice had become an opulent city. The middle classes, who had grown rich on trade, and the great noble families now

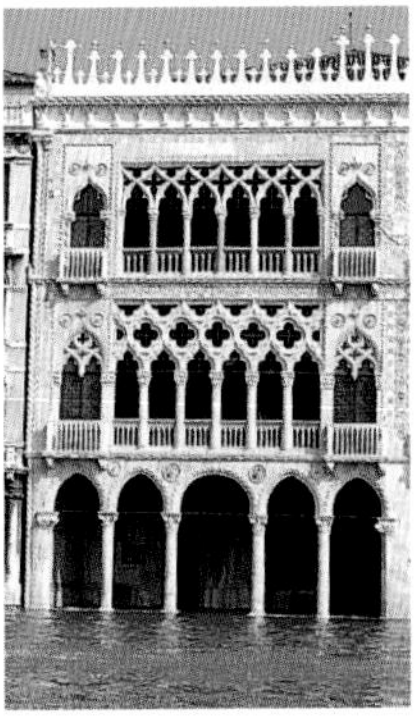

wanted more comfortable, better-lit residences. The most sumptuous of them all, the Ca' d'Oro, displays the characteristics that were all the rage at that time. Its façade (which was originally covered in gold) opens onto the Grand Canal by means of intertwined Gothic arches resembling lacy ribbons, and ornate windows that catch the light. Everywhere you look, fine decoration accentuates the slender lines of the palace and adds to its elegance.

Renaissance harmony

Monumentality, symmetry and harmony were the keywords of Renaissance architecture. The 16th-century palaces, such as Palazzo Vendramin Calergi (the site of the winter casino) and Palazzo Corner, both of which are located on the Grand Canal, were built in brick instead of sandstone. They therefore presented an imposing façade embellished by the horizontal and vertical lines of cornices and pilasters (antique columns). The windows opened onto balconies and had exchanged their broken arcading for round arches.

Baroque style

The Baroque taste for the theatrical triumphed on the Grand Canal with Ca' Pesaro, the palace built by Baldassare Longhena in the mid-17th century. Unlike his Renaissance counterparts, the architect did not leave a single surface of the building unadorned. A profusion of garlands, trophies, monstrous faces and diamond-shaped bosses enlivened the whole of the façade, which gave the palace an unrivaled degree of opulence.

THE STRUCTURE OF THE PALACES AND HOUSES

While the façades of the *palazzi* (the Ca', the diminutive of *casa*, or 'house' in Italian), on which every care was lavished, evolved and followed the dictates of fashion, their internal structure changed little over the centuries. Three floors were more or less the rule up to the 18th century. The first floor, which was accessible by boat, housed stores and a large central space (the *portego*). The second floor (*piano nobile*) was reserved for offices and, in the grand palaces, sumptuously decorated reception rooms. The patrician families lived on the airier third floor and the servants lived in the attic. Venetian residences were grouped around a courtyard, which provided essential ventilation. The courtyard was square in the Middle Ages, but rectangular in shape from the Renaissance onward. It was extended on the side by a *rio* or *calle*.

Marbled paper and stationery

Less than 50 years after the discovery of the printing press, Venice had become the European capital of printing, thanks to the efforts of the humanist printer, Alde Manuce (1449–1515), who invented italic letters. Ink, pens and the famous marbled paper are still made in the city by craftsmen today.

A history of marbled paper

The existence of marbled paper was first documented in Japan in the 13th century. Later, in the 15th and 16th centuries, the technique spread to Persia and then to Turkey, where it was called *ebrû*, after the floral design produced to this day by the *legatoria* of Alberto Valese (see p. 120). Around the 18th century, Western bookbinders used marbled paper *en masse* to cover books. Calfskin had become too expensive and was now only used for the spines, while the flyleaves were covered in paper.
It became such a craze that craftsmen used it to make a wide variety of objects, including boxes of every possible shape and size – a tradition that the craftsmen of Venice have preserved to this day.

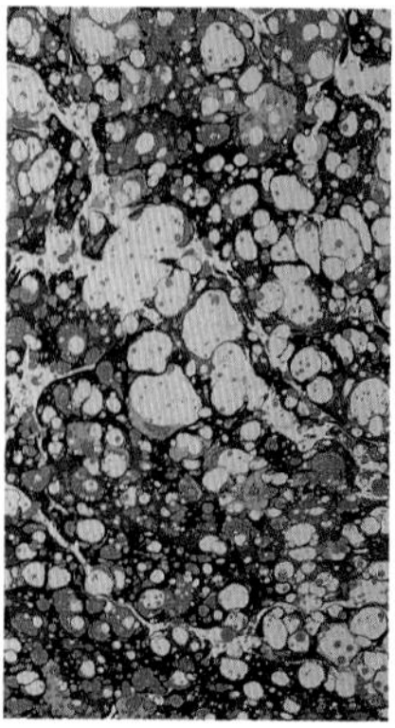

Marbled papermaking

Imagine a drop of colored oil floating on the surface of water. If a sheet of paper is placed delicately on top of it, the color is transferred onto the paper, leaving the water clear. This is the basic principle of marbled papermaking. The craftsman throws drops of color mixed with oxgall into a marbling tank. The drops spread over the surface of the water, which is denser. He then repeats the process with the next color in order to create veining. Once this delicate preparation is complete (the more colors there are, the more likely they are to smudge), he creates designs with a brush or gently "drags" the colors using a point or a comb, in order to obtain lines and swirls. He next places a

sheet of paper on the surface of the water, which becomes impregnated with the pigments in the color bath. All he then has to do is leave it to dry before starting all over again from square one.

How to tell the papers apart

There are several different types of marbled paper:
Pebbled: the colors are not combed, and the pebbling (involving two or three colors) resembles cell tissue as seen under a microscope.
Marbled: as its name suggests, this design resembles marble with veining of one or more colors. This elegant paper is suitable for bookbinding.
Partridge eye and peacock feather marbling: two shimmering designs often involving four colors that are reminiscent of the birds they are named after. These designs are the most difficult to produce because of the danger of the colors mingling.
Ebrû: the craftsman draws floral designs, and the marbled paper produced is probably the most beautiful of all. It is also the design that depends most on the individual creativity of the craftsman.

PENS, INK AND SEALS

Now that we live in the paperback era, marbled papermakers have been forced to supplement their income by adding other strings to their bow. They have extended their skill as printers to the production of distinctive business cards, seals, tarot cards and pens. Delicate and colorful penholders, often made of Murano glass, are sold alongside nibs and handmade writing paper. The ink (of every conceivable color), leaves no deposit, which is a sure sign of quality. Many well-known writers, who number among the city's most ardent fans, swear by these products.

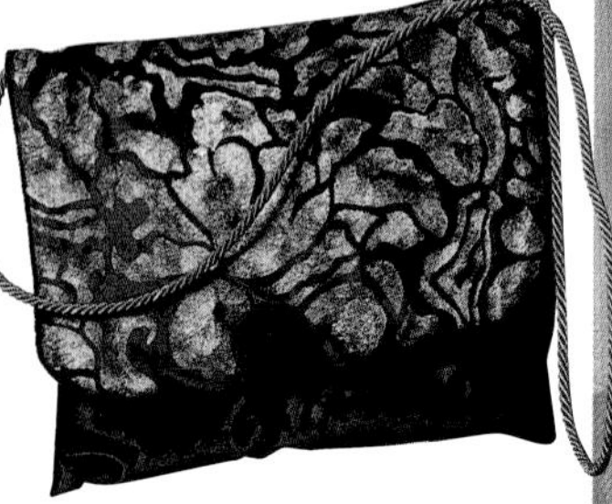

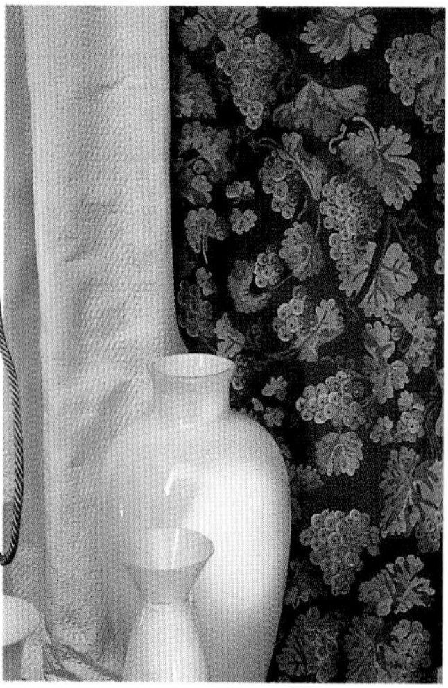

Venetian fabrics

Since the age when Venice was the nerve center of European trade, it has remained the home of luxury fabrics. The incredibly sumptuous hand-printed damasks, silks and brocades that you'll find in the city – some of which are handwoven – are sure to dazzle you with their beauty.

Fortuny, Andalusian turned Venetian

Mariano Fortuny y Madrazo (1871–1949) settled in Venice in 1888, in Palazzo Pesaro degli Orfei. He set up a workshop on the second floor and indulged his passion for the theater and stage costumes in particular. He designed the Cnossos scarf in 1906, and his first Delphos dress the following year, a clinging taffeta garment reminiscent of the charioteer of Delphi. Fortuny later designed a famous lamp (see box opposite) and a whole range of pleated velvets and silk or cotton garments that emphasized the figure and profoundly influenced fashion at the start of the 20th century.

Fortuny pleats

The pleats are made by hand in damp fabric, then sewn in place and fixed with a hot iron. To preserve them, the silk is twisted into skeins. Examples of this technique (scarves in particular) can be seen in the window of Venetia Studium (see p. 111), whose creations use Fortuny's technique to the letter.

The designs

Fortuny used écru-colored velvet or cotton, which he brushed with metallic colors to add a base tone. The designs, which took their inspiration from the Orient, and above all from the Venetian Renaissance, were then stenciled on. They were sometimes combined with a fine network of gold or silver thread. All the Fortuny fabric designs produced on the island of the Giudecca can be found at the shop Vittorio Trois (see p. 111). Other major manufacturers, including Gaggio (see p. 110), also produce hand-printed designs reminiscent of those of Fortuny.

Silk and velvet weaving

The silk damasks and sumptuous iridescent velvets of the firm Rubelli (see p. 110) and the house of Bevilacqua (see p. 110) – the two big names in Venetian fabrics – are made on antique looms dating from as far back as the 18th century. To give an idea of the work involved, a weaver and her assistant only manage to make a strip 40cm (15¾in) long by 60cm (23½in) wide in a day (the maximum allowed by a hand loom).

This goes some way to explain the high price of these fabrics. The other silks and velvets, which are sold in a standard width of 130cm (51in), are made on mechanical looms and are therefore far less expensive.

Affordable accessories

Most of the fabric manufacturers of Venice sell small items made of handprinted silk or velvet. These are the things to go for if you want to bring a little Venetian chic back with you. There are beautiful small purses by Bevilacqua or sumptuous pleated velvet scarves by Venetia Studium for women, and fabulous ties at Gaggio which make perfect gifts for men.

FORTUNY LAMPSHADES

Venetia Studium (see p. 111) is the only place where you can still buy lamps like the ones made by Mariano Fortuny. The silk is placed on the metal frames of the lampshades, then decorated with delicate hand-painted floral designs using gold, silver and other sumptuous colors. The edges are then decorated with Murano hand-blown glass beads. The lamps take a team of a dozen craftsmen several days to make, which puts their high prices somewhat into perspective.

The birth of Venice

Created from mud, built on water, illuminated by an exceptional destiny, Venice made itself a Republic when the rest of Europe only knew monarchies or empires. What's more, it succeeded in maintaining its independence and its might for a thousand years.

In the beginning, marshes

In the 5th century, the beginning did not bode well. To flee Attila's army, the people who would later become Venetians find refuge in the lagoon, a vast expanse of briny water. The marshes surounding Murano, Burano and the Rialto archipelago represent a natural rampart offering as much a deterrent as a town-wall. Who, then, could have imagined that out of this insalubrious site would emerge a prodigious city-state.

Dominating the Adriatic

The inhabitants drain the marshes, develop fishing and trade. Venice conquers the Dalmatian coast, Crete, Cyprus, Genoa, its rival, Verona, Padua, Damascus… Its empire stretches as far as the Black Sea and Constantinople. It rules supreme over the Adriatic and the maritime traffic between the East and the West. An international power, Venice mints its own currency, appoints its own bishops, invents the lazaret and the quarantine. Its expansion slows down after a harsh war against Genoa (1378–1381), the great plague of the 14th century and the fall of the Byzantine empire (1453), when the Turks recapture Constantinople. Meanwhile, Christopher Columbus lands in America in 1492, Portugal, France and England expand rapidly. The Most Serene city, still present and strong, will take part in all the conflicts of the 15th century, but its political decline has begun.

The Republic of Venice (697–1797)

The institutions of Venice were established around 1300. Only the nobility, the families of rich shipowners, merchants or the most deserving representatives of the people

took part in political life. The ducal palace (Doges' Palace) is the epicentre of administration and power and houses the Doge's residence, the rooms of the Grand Council, the Ducal Council and the Council of Ten, the tribunal and the prison. The Doge, who was elected or chosen by drawing lots, is assisted and watched over by a Great Council whose members (as many as 2,000) are elected by 12 electors, two for each district of the city – San Marco, Cannaregio, San Polo. The Great Council controls the city and appoints the senators. A Ducal Council, assisting the Doge, is composed of six members without whose opinion the Doge cannot do anything, let alone disregard the decisions of the Great Council. In the 14th century, the redoutable Council of the Ten was even put in charge of foiling plots against the state. Power is not in the hands of the doges. The laws, the multitude of offices and the complexity with which they were attributed stifle as much any attempt at tyranny or at scheming among the elected members and the doges as the people's desire for rebellion. However, the leaders of this unique system, both democratic and elitist, who have come out of the *comitia* representing the people (who are not allowed citizenship) do conduct a coherent social policy, encourage hygiene and assistance to the poor. The non-religious *scuole* (schools) will play an important part in culture and charity.

From Bonaparte... to tourism

In the 18th century, despite the decline of Venice, elegant palaces are still being built, people continue to celebrate, the artistic Renaissance is at its pinacle and the city-state is still impressive. In 1797, after a short-lived invasion by the French, when the town surrendered meekly to Bonaparte, the Republic of Venice is dissolved and through the Campoformio treaty, the whole territory is given over to Austria. In 1866, Venetia is returned to the Kingdom of Italy. Today, tourism and the petrochemical industry in Porto Marghera enable Venice to prosper.

THE PATRON SAINT OF VENICE

According to the long and flourishing history of the Doges' city, Saint Mark, whose symbolic animal in the Bible is the lion, was and remains an effective patron saint. It is rumored that the relics of the evangelist, the first bishop of Alexandria (where he was tortured and buried in 67) were brought back to the Serenissima in 828, hidden in the carcass of a salt pork by two Venetian merchants.

Carnivals and regattas

The Doges' city likes grand spectacle! The Biennale, an exhibition of contemporary art, the Mostra, wild regattas, colorful religious festivals and the famous Carnival, despite the latter having lost some of its traditional folly.

TO NOTE

The Cini Foundation, Correr Museum, Grassi and Fortuny palaces often hold remarkable temporary exhibitions. Find out at the tourist office or simply look at the posters up around town.

Religious festivals and regattas

Festival of the Ascension *(festa della Sensa)*

On Ascension Day (*Sensa*), a notable of the city perpetuates the Doges' custom of throwing a gold ring and laurel wreath into the water as a token of union with the sea.

Festival of the Redeemer *(festa del Redentore)*

The Festival of the Redeemer, commemorating the end of the plague of 1576, takes place in the third week in July. A bridge formed by a number of boats joins Salute and Venice opposite. There is a marvelous firework display.

Historic regattas *(Regata storica)*

These regattas are held on the first Sunday in September, and have been taking place since the 12th century. Spectators gather on the banks of the Grand Canal and on the Ponte di Rialto and Ponte dell'Accademia to watch the boat procession. Then it's time

Procession of the Doge in Saint Mark's Square, *Giovanni Bellini (1470).*

for the highlight of the festival, the two-oar gondola race, which arouses the passion of the crowds.

The Vagalonga

The Sunday following Ascension Day is the day of the Vagalonga, an endurance race involving hundreds of boats. The 30km (19 mile) race from Venice to Burano and back again via the Cannaregio Canal is cheered wildly by the waiting crowds.

The Festival of the Salute *(festa della Madonna della Salute)*

Every November 21, in memory of a vow made during the plague epidemic of 1631, a procession of the faithful sets off from the Basilica San Marco, crosses the floating bridge built for the occasion over the Grand Canal, and makes its way to S. Maria della Salute to ask the Virgin to keep them in good health.

The arts

The Biennale, an exhibition of contemporary art, has been in existence since 1895. Usually held on odd years, generally from mid-June to the beginning of November, it is a gathering place for hundreds of artists and around sixty countries. The works of art (paintings, sculptures, videos, etc.) are displayed in the magnificent pavilions of the Giardini, inside the Castello. On average 250,000 visitors come through its doors. In the same venue (on even years) and in the same spirit, the Biennial of architecture takes place from mid-September to early November.
The international festival of contemporary music offers various musical experiences for about ten days in October. Concerts are usually given at the Malibran theater, in the Fenice or at the Piccolo Arsenale theater. Finally, new since 2003, the international festival of contemporary dance is deliberately geared toward avant-garde dance styles. In June and July.

Information: ☎ 041 24 24 or www.labiennale.org

THE VENETIAN MOSTRA

This great movie festival is held for two weeks at the Lido between the end of August and mid-September. Movies are shown in the main hall of the imposing Palazzo del Cinema and also at the Astra theater. What a dream it would be to attend the prize giving ceremony of the Golden Lion and Silver Lion or any of the previews, unless of course you are one of the happy few who are connected to the world of moviemaking! If you are staying in Venice during the Mostra, it is still worth hurrying over to the Lido and positioning yourself on one of the strategic terraces of the Lungomare Marconi. You will be able to spot the budding new Mastroiannis who stroll on the waterfront.

For the Mostra addresses, see p. 131.
Information: ☎ 041 24 24 or www.labiennale.org

The Carnival

In the past, the Carnival used to be the last festival authorized by the church before the start of Lent. It literally means "farewell to the flesh" (*carne levare* to remove the meat). The Venice Carnival takes place over the ten days preceding Ash Wednesday (first two weeks of February), when it becomes impossible to find a room in Venice without reserving several months in advance. It is so busy that sometimes you can't even reach the city by road! The Venice Carnival started in the 10th or 11th century and reached its heyday in the 17th century. At that time, the festivities lasted nearly half a year, from October to Lent. The wearing of masks blurred the sexes, negated social differences and allowed every folly. It was forbidden to forbid, and Casanovas threw eggshells filled with perfume under ladies' windows. Others, who were far more subversive, organized balls in the convents. The Carnival was suspended in 1797, at the end of the Republic, and wasn't started again until 1979, at the instigation of an association of Venetian citizens. At first, in the early 1980s, it was spontaneous and inventive, but it became such a huge success that the tourists began to arrive in droves. The Venetians have gradually abandoned the congested *calle* to the foreigners and withdrawn to the heart of the palaces and theaters. It's there, and in certain *campi* far removed from Piazza San Marco, that the Carnival comes into its own.

The different costumes

Tarocco outfits are reminiscent of the figures featured on tarot cards used in fortune-telling. They're the favorite costumes of Venetians and elegant tourists alike. However, they're closely followed in the popularity stakes by the *maschera nobile,* the Carnival outfit of aristocrats in the 18th century. This is made up of the traditional *bauta* (a white mask that appeared in the late 18th century), the *tabarro* (a short cape) and the famous black cocked hat.

The characters of the Commedia dell'Arte

Each of the stock characters of the Commedia dell'Arte was the incarnation of a human vice or form of ridicule. They were immediately recognizable to the audience by their silhouettes and masks (although the female characters – Colombine, Isabella and Silvia – didn't wear masks). The following

are the most popular costumes you'll come across in the streets of Venice during the Carnival.
Harlequin: Pantalone's valet, Arlecchino, wears a diamond-patterned outfit (red, orange and green) and a black mask. He was originally coarse and cynical before becoming a comical acrobat and, later, in the works of Marivaux, a naive, sensitive servant.
Brighella: Pantalone's manservant and the personification of treachery, Brighella uses and abuses stratagems to achieve his ends. He wears a white

costume with diagonal green stripes and a green mask with a broken nose that makes him look rather frightening.
The Doctor: Il Dottore is a lawyer and a typical man of letters; he's both talkative and pretentious. He wears knee-stockings, black breeches and a black cape over a white shirt and ruff; his mask has a prominent forehead and a big nose.
Pantalone: an old skinflint who's also passionately in love; he's the favorite butt of the servants' joke. He wears black pants and a mask with a mustache embellished with a long hooked nose.
Pulcinella: a lovable comical character dressed in white who wears a black mask with a hooked nose. In Italy, Pulcinella isn't a hunchback, unlike the French Polichinelle (Punch).
Scaramouche: subtle and boastful, he's dressed in black and hides behind a black mask with a flat nose.

HOW A MASK IS MADE

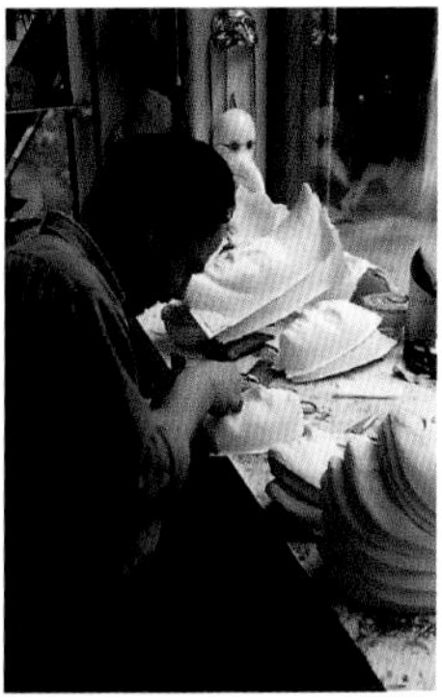

The mask maker first shapes the mask out of clay, then pours plaster into it to make a mold. This fragile plaster shell is lined with a papier-mâché mixture made from paper, rags and glue, and is then left to dry. After removing the mask from the mold, the craftsman polishes its surface and carefully trims it, which involves cutting out the eyes, mouth, etc. A coat of white primer is then applied to the finished mask, which is finally painted by hand. Leather masks (considerably more expensive) can take various shapes (characters from the Commedia dell'Arte, double masks, baroque masks in the shape of the moon or the sun, etc.). The craftsman softens the leather to work on its shape. He then applies gold leaf or color to the mask, according to his imagination. A leather mask is even more valuable if it is made out of one single piece. To find out, turn it over!

The finer points of lacemaking

Legend has it that one fine day, a sailor gave his love a strange marine plant, *Halynedia opuntia*, which is more commonly known as "mermaids' lace." When he had left on his voyage, the young woman did her best to reproduce the plant using only her needle. She thus invented the *punto in aria* (needlepoint), which is derived from the technique for making fishing nets. Today, only a handful of Burano lacemakers are willing to "ruin their eyesight" with the difficult art of Venetian *merletto*.

Burano lace and Venetian lace

Venetian lace is a linen fabric made with a needle (*ad ago*) rather than a bobbin (*a fuseli*). The background and the flowers, or *ornaments*, are formed by the lacemaker over a paper pattern fixed to a cushion.

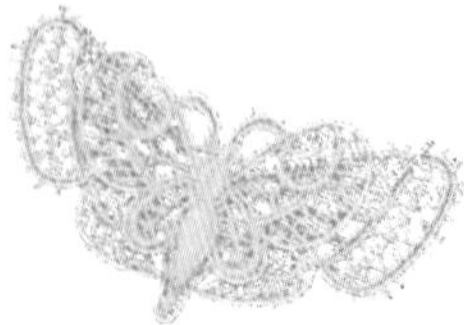

This *punto in aria* (needlepoint), invented around 1540, first involves the construction of a grid or framework. It's this that makes all the difference between Venetian *merletto* and simple embroidery, which

requires a foundation to support the work. The lace found in Venice is either Burano lace or Venetian lace. Burano lace is easily recognizable by its background of square stitches and its transparency. It's the most delicate and also the most expensive, and can only be found at Jesurum (see p. 116). Venetian lace, unashamedly copied by the Colbert lace of Bayeux, has a background consisting

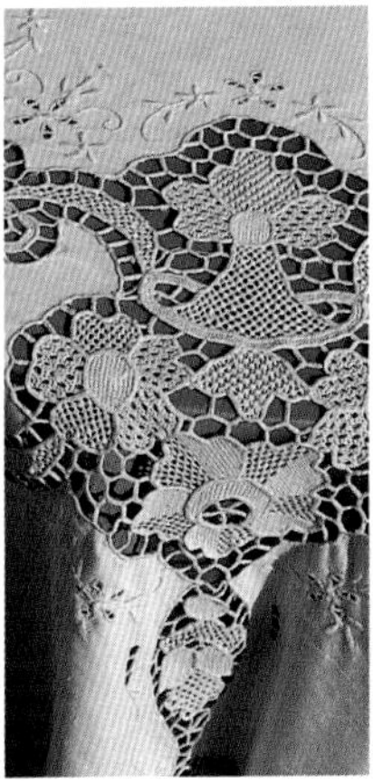

of bars or 'brides' (overcast bars of thread). It's a play on relief and allows lacemakers to make very complex designs. Along with the bobbin lace made along the coast (at Chioggia and Pellestrina), this is the best type of lace you can buy in the shops of Burano.

A short history of lacemaking

Lace has been popular in Venice since the early Middle Ages, and by the 16th century it was no longer reserved for vestments only. It had also found its way onto blouses and dresses, and later onto men's clothes, fans, sheets, curtains and even shoes. When Louis IV's minister, Colbert, set up a lace factory in France in the 17th century, it dealt a heavy blow to Venetian production as the best Burano lacemakers left the island in answer to his call. Around 1750, Venice responded by setting up its own factories,

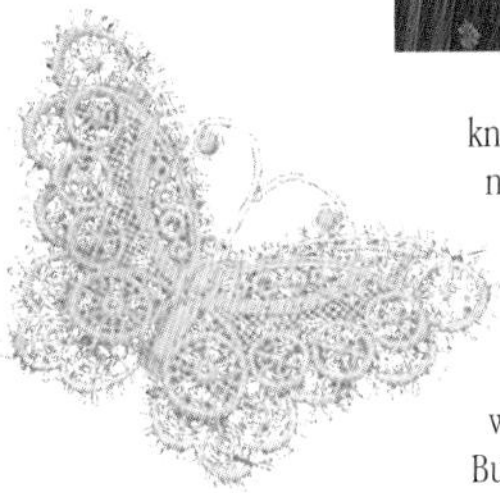

but skilled workers became more and more difficult to find. In 1872 there was only one woman who still knew how to make needlepoint lace. It was she who taught in the lacemaking school – Scuola dei merletti – which opened in Burano. Nowadays, almost the entire output of the last remaining lacemakers is sold by the Jesurum shop.

LACEMAKING IN THE AGE OF COMPUTERS

Lacemaking is a very labor-intensive process. A hand-embroidered linen tablecloth represents three years' work and even a simple design involves the labor of seven women (from conception to finished product). All this must be paid for and it doesn't come cheap. Since the 1980s, computers have played a part in helping to bring down the cost of lacemaking. Software has been developed that makes it possible to copy and modify any design. The designs are transferred to cards, stored in memory and executed by machines that can do the equivalent of a day's work by hand in less than an hour. You can find machine embroidery produced in this way (made in Taiwan or Singapore) on sale at tempting prices in many of the shops of Burano.

Murano:
transparency and color

From the Renaissance to the great figures of the 20th century, including Archimede Seguso, Ermanno Toso, Ercole Barovier and Paolo Venini, the master glassmakers of Murano have never ceased to develop and improve an art that remains forever linked with the name of Venice.

The history of Murano glass

Glass has been made in Venice since as long ago as the 10th century, but the craft only took off with the arrival of Byzantine glassmakers following the sack of Constantinople in 1204. The Doges soon moved the guild's kilns to the island of Murano. Officially, this was to protect the city from fire; however, it is more likely that the Serenissima was seeking to protect itself from competition. Its master glassmakers were forbidden to share their secrets or further foreign initiatives in any way whatsoever. Offenders immediately had their property confiscated and could even be sentenced to death. In the 15th and 16th centuries, master glassmakers invented colored glass and refined their techniques. They created new shapes of vase, and designed chandeliers and mirrors. Venetian production began to show signs of decline in the 17th century, when it was faced with competition from Bohemian glass, and later, in the 19th century, with the success of crystal.

Murano glassmaking

Various ingredients are used to obtain the vitrifiable raw material based on siliceous sand or silica (70% of the mixture by weight). The mixture is heated to 1,400°C/2500°F, before the temperature is lowered to 1,000°C/1800°F to allow the glassblower to carry out his work. On the end of a hollow rod, he picks up some molten

glass and rotates it in a mold to obtain a ball. He blows briefly down the rod and turns it rapidly in order to prevent the ball at the end from stretching. After pinching the base, he blows again before piercing the ball with a sharp point. He then shapes the glass to give it its curved form. Once this is complete, the glass is again heated before being placed in a kiln kept at a lower temperature.

THE MURANO YOU WILL SEE

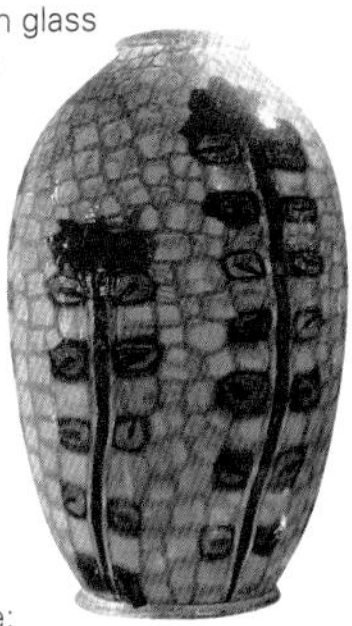

Aventurine: translucent brown glass with inclusions of very brilliant copper crystals.
Cristallino: glass resembling rock crystal made from silica and manganese. This technique, which was invented by the master glassmaker Angelo Barovier (1405–1460), made the Murano glass famous.
Lattimo: glass that imitates porcelain *(porcellana contraffatta)* whose opacity is due to the addition of tin oxide; the designation *lattimo* also covers colorless glass with white inclusions.
Millefiori: the assembly of small pieces of colored glass to create a design; the whole thing is then melted in order to make the pieces stick together.
Lead glass: inexpensive glass that's far softer than the *cristallino* type; it's used to do enamel work and to make the lengths of glass from which Murano beads are made.
Lace glass: a technique invented in 1527; colored or enameled straws are included in colorless molten glass.
***Ghiaccio* glass:** a technique invented around 1570 where frozen water is added to the vitrified paste; the temperature difference creates an undulating pattern that gives the glass the appearance of melted ice.
Cut glass: glass with designs (often floral) drawn with diamond tips.

Venetian furniture

The whole of Europe has long admired the furniture and mirrors made by the Venetian cabinetmakers and Murano glass-makers. Resplendent with Baroque gilding, Chinese lacquer and translucent colors, these works of art form an integral part of the Venetian landscape.

Mirrors

The oldest mirrors you'll see in the palaces date from the 16th century. They have heavy walnut frames and resemble small altarpieces. In the following century they acquired cut-glass pediments that were often blue in color. Mirrors with a gilded wooden frame flourished in the 18th century, when Rococo was all the rage. This type of mirror, with its ornate molding using a theme of plants, can be found (along with 19th-century pastiches) in the large antique shops of the city, but they cost a small fortune and can fetch thousands of dollars at auction outside Italy. In the late 18th century, wooden molding covered in gold leaf gradually disappeared, except on mirrors destined for the decoration of the great palaces. From then on, the borders were made of engraved glass, decorated with spun glass, colorful Murano glass flowers or polychrome earthenware from Bassano. These types of mirror are also well represented in the large antique shops, and the shops on Murano sell more or less successful modern copies of them.

Fine Venetian furniture

It was in Venice that the finest Italian furniture of the 18th century was produced. In style,

it was Louis XV, Louis XVI or Chippendale (Rococo enriched with designs influenced by Chinese, Japanese or Gothic art). Most of this furniture was made from lacquered walnut decorated with floral motifs. Some of the furniture is noteworthy. For example, the **pedestal desk** is a desk whose upper part acts as a small bookcase; the Venetian vogue for this item of furniture can be in part explained by the importance of writing and printing in the city.
The **chair** was a great speciality of the cabinetmakers of the Serenissima; Venetian chairs can be distinguished from their English counterparts by the caning and the use of Chinese or Japanese lacquers.
The **sofa** was an Italian invention (17th century). The sofa took on vast proportions in Venice as elsewhere; the finest had openwork embroidery backs.
The **chest of drawers,** potbellied as the period required, were lacquered in a pale shade and highly decorated with Rococo motifs.
The originality of the **armchair** resided in its three carved walnut feet; some armchairs that were lacquered and embellished with precious reliefs were works of art in themselves.
Finally, the **console table,** with its undulating top surmounted by a fabulous Murano glass mirror, was used as a tidy by the nobility.
To find these pieces, visit the many antique shops.
Or visit the Ca' Rezzonico, museum of 17th-century Venice, where you will find some extremely rare pieces of furniture.

Tempted to buy?

Check the hinges carefully (they're always imperfect because they're handmade), as well as the roughness of the inner surfaces (wood was once always sawn by hand). Check that old parts haven't been combined with new, artificially aged ones. Finally, look out for that classic – buckshot made to look like woodworm. You should scarcely be able to stick a needle into the hole (the tunnel dug by a worm is winding, not straight).

THE SECONDHAND MARKETS

Some say there are no longer bargains to be had at the Campo S. Maurizio secondhand market (see p. 45). If you're really mad about antiques, go to the far less well-known market in Jesolo in July and August (*vaporetto* 14 to Punta Sabbioni, then a taxi).
There's also another interesting market in Corso del Popolo in Mestre (frequent trains from Lucia station) the first weekend in every month (except July and August). Be vigilant at all times wherever you are – tourists are considered easy prey here. Bargain hard and read carefully the few basic "rules" for telling the real from the fake before buying anything.

The flavors of Venice

Fish and polenta are the main ingredients of Venetian gastronomy. Vegetables, pasta and Eastern influence further enrich the large and generous range of Mediterrean flavors. Pastries are not neglected either.

Healthy and diverse

Famous writers, starting with Goldoni and Casanova, have mentioned Venetian cuisine and alluded to its Oriental influence and spicy, sweet-and-sour (*all'agro*) flavors. Olive oil, onions, rice, almonds, pine nuts and dried fruit on the one hand, home-grown vegetables (peas, beans, asparagus, artichokes, endives and zucchini) on the other.

How to make polenta

This grilled corn meal, which is usually yellow in color, but sometimes white, is the main accompaniment to a large number of Venetian dishes (cod dish in particular, *baccalà mantecato*). It's very easy to make. For 3 people, add 250g (8¾oz) of cornflour to a liter (1¾pt) of boiling salted water and cook for 30 mins (or more, for an even better flavor), stirring the mixture the whole time. Pour into a greased mold and leave to cool. Cut into rectangles and finally brown under a grill.

Dishes to try in Venice

Starters

Zuppa di pesce: a delicious saffron-flavored fish soup.
Fiori di zucchini: zucchini-flower fritters stuffed with fish mousse.
Risi e bisi: a pea and rice-based dish (sometimes flavored with bacon).
Risotto alle seppie: rice

with Parmesan and cuttlefish ink.

Vegetables
Fagioli in saor: large marinated beans.
Melanzane in saor: marinated eggplants.

In saor
This marinade, made with white wine vinegar, onions, pine kernels and raisins, is used as an accompaniment to vegetables (beans or *fagioli*) and mainly fish (the famous *sarde* or sardines *in saor*)

Pasta
Parpadelle col radicchio: large flat pasta with grilled red endives from Treviso, garlic and onions.
Bigoli in salsa: a kind of thick wholemeal spaghetti cooked in a sauce made with onion and anchovies.
Spaghetti ai carciofi: spaghetti with artichokes.

Meat and fish
Anguilla in umido: eel in tomato sauce with white wine and garlic.
Bacalà mantecato: a typical cod dish with parsley and olives.
Seppie in tecia: cuttlefish in white wine with tomato and basil.

Confectionery
Amaretti: small almond-flavored cakes to eat with coffee.
Baute: colorful chocolates that are found all over the city.
Croccantini: nougat eaten with sweet wine in bistrots.
Essi buranelli: S-shaped egg cookies (when ring-shaped, they're known as *bussolai buranelli*).
Fritoli: hot donuts with currants served during the Carnival.
Galani: small cakes that are fried and sprinkled with sugar; they're eaten at Carnival time and are also called *crostoli*.
Tiramisù: a delicious cake made from cookies sprinkled with amaretto, and almond and coffee-flavored mascarpone, all sprinkled with chocolate powder.
Zaeti: small cornflour rolls sprinkled with confectioners' sugar.

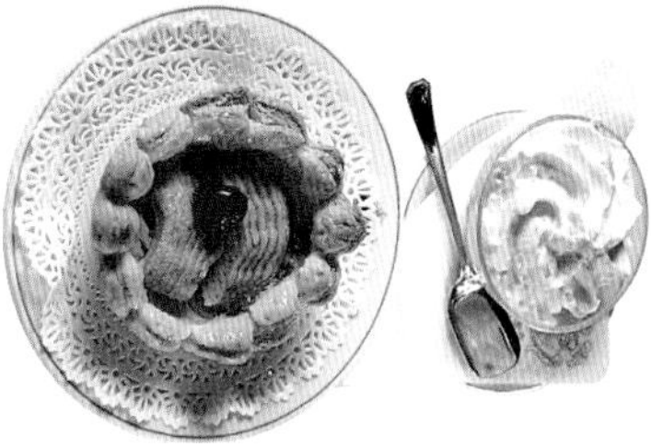

A VENETIAN MENU

Hors-d'œuvre: *carpaccio* (thin slices of beef marinated in oil).
Primo piatto: *spaghetti alle vongole* (with cockles) or *alle seppie* (with squid ink).
Secondo piatto: *sarde in saor* (sardines marinated in onions, vinegar and pine kernels, then grilled), *baccalà mantecato* (mashed cod with oil, garlic and parsley) or *fegato alla veneziana* (calf's liver on a bed of onions).
Contorno: *polenta* (flat cake made with cornflour).
Dessert: *tiramisù*.

Bardolino, Valpolicella and grappa

Venetia produces eleven DOC (*Denominazione di origine controllata*, or *appellation contrôlée*) wines and a countless number of local (IT or *Indicazione tipica*) wines and table wines. To these must be added all the many varieties of grappa, or brandy, made from the best wines of the region.

The wine regions

The Venetian wines come from the Verona region (around Lake Garda) and Vicenze (west of Venice), or north of Treviso (the Piave valley). They represent 13 percent of the entire wine production of Italy, putting Venetia in third place behind Sicily and Apulia.

The wines of the Verona region: Bardolino, Soave and Valpolicella

These are the best wines of Venetia. They're exported abroad in vast quantities and wine lovers will almost certainly be familiar with them. They come from the shores of Lake Garda northwest of Verona.
Bardolino (a small town on the southeast of Lake Garda) wine comes as either *chiaretto* (rosé) or *classico* (red). It's marvelous chilled with meat and cheese.
Soave *classico* is a smooth, fairly robust white wine that goes well with white meat and fish. It's the fourth most exported Italian wine.

Valpolicella (the fifth most exported Italian wine) is a full-bodied red. It can be drunk at room temperature or chilled. It comes in two forms: Valpolicella classico or, better still, Valpolicella superiore.

The other labels

The Verona region produces three other appellation contrôlée wines that you can try: Bianco di Custoza, a white wine that should be drunk chilled with meals or as an aperitif; Gambellara, a light, dry wine (red or white); and Valdadige (red, rosé or white), which is produced on the banks of the Adige.

The Treviso region

The best wine of the region is **Prosecco**, a sparkling wine (very dry, dry or medium dry) produced from the vines on the hills of Conegliano and Valdobbiadene, north of Treviso. The Venetians drink it as an aperitif. Those in the know swear by the Prosecco of Cartizze, which has the richest flavor. Prosecco also exists in the form of a classic white wine and a *frizzante*.

The other labels

Other wines of the Treviso region have been designated DOC (appellation contrôlée): Colli di Conegliano, a smooth, very robust red or white wine; Montello e Colli Asolani, red, white, or *spumante* varieties, with just a hint of almonds; and finally Piave, red or white, but the least good and held in low esteem by wine connoisseurs.

Wine terms

Amabile: medium dry
Bianco: white
Classico: standard quality
Frizzante: slightly sparkling
Rosso: red
Secco: dry
Spumante: sparkling
Superiore: superior quality

Grappa

Brandy, or grappa, (around 40°) is produced throughout northern Italy. A little drop in your coffee (order a *coretto)* will certainly set you up for a rigorous day's sightseeing in the city. In Venetia, the best grappa is made from Prosecco or Valpolicella. The most famous is the Nardini.

Italian aperitifs and liqueurs

Spritz is the typical Venetian aperitif. You can also have a famous Campari, a Cynar (bitter, with an artichoke aftertaste) or an alcohol-free Crodino.The great liqueurs of the region are Amaretto (a 24-28° liqueur which has an almond flavor and is made from apricot stones) and Amari (a bitter liqueur around 45°, made from the bark and roots of various plants).

WHERE TO TASTE AND BUY WINE

If you want to taste the different varieties of Venetian wine, go to an *osteria-enoteca*: Harry's Bar, Al Volto, Vino Vino, Vini da Pinto, Già Schiavi et Mascareta (see pp. 94–95, 96). To buy wine, see the places listed on pp. 126–127.

Practicalities

Getting around

The different islands are well served, but in Venice itself, which is not so big after all, the simplest means of transportation is often to get around… on foot! There is no precise map of Venice, but it is easy to find one's way around, to find the *bacaro* or the store you are looking for: the Venetians know their town by heart.

The streets of Venice

A street is not always called a *calle*. According to its location, its shape and its history the term changes. Thus a *calle* becomes a *fondamenta* when it runs along a canal, a *piscina* when it used to shelter a water tank or a basin, a *ramo* when it is bent at an angle. A *rio terà* means you are walking on an ancient canal which is today filled in, a *ruga* is a shopping street, a *salizzada* a cobbled street, and a *sottoportico* a covered alley.

By boat

You can either take the *vaporetto* or the *motoscafo*. The former is big, rather slow, and offers fine vistas of Venice from its open deck. The latter is low over the water and faster, with a smaller deck. You can use it to go to the islands of the lagoon (Murano, Burano and Torcello). The *motonave*, a kind of large ferry boat, only serves the parts of Venice where cars are allowed, especially the Lido.
– The central lines (1, 3, 4 and

"VISIT VENICE" PACKAGES

– The Venice Card exists in two different colors : blue and orange. The former enables you to use public transportation and rest rooms free of charge. The latter includes the entrance fee to some museums or offers a slight reduction. They are valid from 1 to 7 days (from €14 to €68, to be reserved 48 hours in advance on www.venicecard.it). It is difficult to take full advantage of these two cards over a weekend, even a long one.
– The €8 Chorus card enables you to visit 15 churches (information on www.chorusvenezia.org). You'll be saving money after the fourth church and the card is valid for a year.
– The attractive Museum pass costing €15.5 enables you, among other things, to visit the museums of Piazza San Marco (Palazzo Ducale, Correr Museum), Ca' Rezzonico and Ca' Pesaro, and the museums on the islands (Murano, Burano).
– Information on www.museiciviciveneziani.it.

HOW TO FIND AN ADDRESS

In Venice, an address is made up of a figure followed by the name of the district (S. Marco, Dorsoduro, S. Polo, S. Croce, Cannaregio, Castello, Giudecca, etc.). It's disconcerting at first, but you soon get used to it. Go to the district in question and ask a passer-by for more precise directions. You then simply follow the numbers around to the correct place. If you want to find your way more quickly, you can buy the *Indicatore Anagrafico* (from a bookstore), which gives the names of the streets corresponding to the various numbers.

82) make use of the Grand Canal both ways.
– Lines 41, 42, 51, 52, 61, 62, DM are called "circular": they go around Venice, and some of them go to the islands of Giudecca, Lido or Murano.
– The lagoon lines (5, 11, 13, 17, 18, 20, LN, T, 24) run to the smaller islands such as S. Lazzaro, S. Erasmo, Burano and Chioggia. Line 5 runs directly from San Marco to Murano.
– Take note: a crossed number means that the *vaporetto* only runs for part of the route

Timetables

Generally speaking, the *vaporetto*, *motoscafo* and *motonave* operate from 5am to 12pm. Between 7am and 9pm the average waiting time is 10 or 20 minutes. The night lines (N) link the Venice islands Burano, Murano, Giudecca and Lido together, serve the Venice tour and the Grand Canal. You can expect a 20, 30, up to 60 min. waiting time. The tourist information office sells an "ACTV timetable" (€0.60) with accurate times. Otherwise you can refer to the free weekly *Un Ospite di Venezia* (but it is less exhaustive) or the map of *Leo Bussola* distributed everywhere.

Price of tickets

Tickets can be bought from the booths of the main stations, from the newspaper kiosks and the tobacco shops bearing the initials ACTV. The ticket costs €3.5 (same price on board), €6 for a round-trip ticket on the same day, €5 for the Grand Canal lines, €10.5 for 24h, €22 for 72h. To go to Burano and Torcello, see pp. 70–71. For more information: ☎ 041 24 24, www.hellovenezia.it or www.actv.it.

Traghetti

Aboard spartan gondolas and for next to nothing, you can cross the Grand Canal in eight places (from morning to evening, at the yellow signs). The stations are shown at Vallaresso next to the Palazzo Gritti, the Ca' Rezzonico, at San Tomà, San Silvestro, at the Ca' d'Oro, San Marcuola and Ferrovia.

Gondolas

A trip for two people costs at least €80 for 30 minutes. It's a good idea to agree on the price in advance and worth bargaining for a reduction, especially out of season. There are 12 gondola "stands". The best are: San Marco del Giglio, San Marco, San Tomà and Rialto.

Taxi acquei
In the historic center, a short ride aboard one of these varnished wooden speedboats, from Piazzale Roma to the city center, will cost you at least €40–€50. Prices vary greatly according to the ride and the boatman.
Try bargaining.
At the hotel ask for the telephone number of the nearest terminal or call, for example ☎ 041 522 23 03, ☎ 041 723 112 or ☎ 041 522 12 65.
If you prefer to be independent, you can always rent a speedboat, with or without driver! (Cooperativa San Marco, ☎ 041 522 23 03 or Noleggio Barche Brussa, ☎ 041 71 57 87).

Making a phone call

There are plenty of telephones around (taking cards and more rarely coins). The only problem is that you need to use a flashlight to be able to dial the number at night. A card machine can be found at the Fondaco dei Tedeschi post office (Salizzada Fondacco dei Tedeschi, San Marco, 5554) if the tobacco shops (look for the black "T" sign) have sold out, which is often the case in the city center.

International calls:
To telephone abroad, dial 00 followed by the country code, (Canada/USA 1, UK 44, Aus 61, NZ 64, Ireland 353) then the number you require (without any 0).

Calls within Venice:
Dial the full number (including area code).

Calls to Venice from abroad:
00 + 39 + 041 (area code for Venice) + number.

To make your life simpler, you can use one of the many international phonecards that allow you to dial a toll-free number from any telephone booth, and then charge the call to a prepaid account or credit card. Calls from a hotel are subject to surcharges.

USEFUL NUMBERS

Tourist information:
☎ 041 24 24.

Flight information:
☎ 041 260 92 60.

Consolates:
UK ☎ 041 522 72 07
US (Milan)
☎ 02 290 351

Lost property:
☎ 041 260 92 22.

Emergencies
Ospedale Civile:
Campo S. Giovanni e Paolo
☎ 041 523 00 00.

Night doctor:
☎ 041 529 40 60.

National police:
☎ 113.

Emergency:
☎ 118.

City police:
☎ 112.

Fire:
☎ 115.

Car breakdown (ACI):
☎ 116.

Internet cafés

You will easily be able to find Internet cafés in Venice. They are present nearly everywhere. The going rate is €4 to €5 for a 30-minute connection.

Sending mail

You can buy stamps from tobacco shops or post offices.

You need a 62 cent stamp to send a letter first-class to a country in the European Union and a 80 cent stamp to other countries. The mailboxes are usually red (national and international mail) but sometimes blue (international mail).

Main post office: Fondaco dei Tedeschi (Salizzada Fondaco dei Tedeschi, 5554 San Marco)
☎ 041 271 72 36
Mon.-Fri. 8.30am-6.30pm.

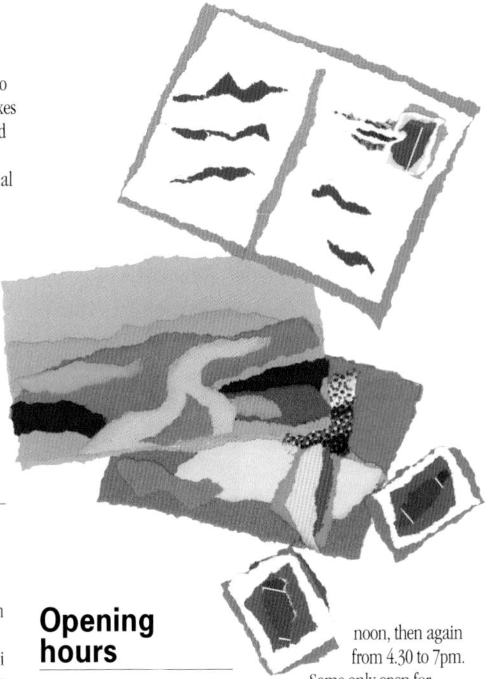

Tourist offices

These are open every day 8.30am-7.30pm (opening times vary according to season), and can be found in various parts of the city: Palazzetto (near the Giardini Reali) and Piazza San Marco (near the Correr Museum).
Stazione S. Lucia (8am-7pm)
☎ 041 529 87 27,
☎ and Ⓕ 041 71 90 78.
Viale S. M. Elisabetta, Lido
☎ 041 526 57 21,
Ⓕ 041 529 87 20.
You can get a map of the city here, as well as a plan of the *vaporetto* network and the indispensable weekly publication *Un Ospite di Venezia* (in Italian and English), which lists exhibitions, concerts and plays and provides lots of practical information, including the opening hours of the city's major monuments. If you come on the spur of the moment, they'll also reserve you a hotel room.

Opening hours

Museums and monuments

The official timetables are unfortunately subject to sudden unexpected changes. The best way to find out when a particular place is open is to pick up a copy of *Un Ospite di Venezia*. As a rough guide, the famous monuments and big museums open from 9/10am to 4pm or even 6/7pm, and small museums and private museums from 9am to 1pm. On Monday they are often, but not always, closed.

Churches

Be prepared for timetables which are even more irregular than those of museums and monuments. In general, there is an entrance fee (€2–€4) and they open every morning until noon, then again from 4.30 to 7pm. Some only open for mass or remain permanently closed, for no apparent reason.

Finding out

The *Gazettino* and *Nuova Venezia* are the two Venetian daily newspapers. They contain useful information (emergency drugstores, weather forecast, etc.) and movie and theater programs. For a kiosk which opens late, go to Folin, San Marco, 1257/A, ☎ 041 522 99 02.

MORE INFORMATION

You'll find route maps for all the walks in this chapter at the head of each tour, and references to sights which also appear in the Don't Miss section.

What to see in Venice
and sights not to miss

To help you to discover the city, we have planned 16 walks in Venice and the surrounding islands, all illustrated by a map. However, if you only have a limited amount of time, here are 12 sights not to be missed. They are all described within this guide at the end of What to See.

Piazza San Marco

The absolute must, Venice's most famous attraction, so full of magical treasures one can never tire of visiting it.

See walk number 1, p. 40 and Don't Miss p. 72.

Basilica San Marco

The San Marco Basilica is teeming with remarkable works of art. One day will hardly suffice to discover all of its treasures.

See walk number 1, p. 40 and Don't Miss p. 73.

Palazzo Ducale

For those who love painting and architecture, this Gothic palace is home to an impressive collection of masterpieces by Veronese and Bassano. Don't miss the famous Bridge of Sighs, which overlooks the canal on one of the palace's sides.

See walk number 1, p. 41 and Don't Miss p. 74.

Palazzo Grassi

The Grassi Palace has much to offer: a fascinating history, its splendid interior decoration and a highly attractive and eclectic program of temporary exhibitions.

See walk number 3, p. 45 and Don't Miss p. 75.

Accademia Gallery

This gallery is housed in one of the world's most beautiful buildings. A must for those who are interested in Venetian painting from the 14th to the 18th centuries. In front of the gallery, the Accademia Bridge offers a fantastic view of the Grand Canal.

See walk number 6, p. 50 and Don't Miss p. 76.

Rio and Squero San Trovaso

A wonderful way of discovering traditional Venice, as you take a stroll through the gondola district.

See walk number 6, p. 51 and Don't Miss p. 77.

Peggy Guggenheim Foundation

In stark contrast with the ancient splendor of the Piazza San Marco and the Accademia gallery, this foundation has a remarkable collection of modern art.

See walk number 7, p. 52 and Don't Miss p. 78.

Santa Maria della Salute

A beautiful Baroque church whose location on the tip of the Dorsoduro district, right where the Grand and the Giudecca canals meet, offers one of the most beautiful views of the city.

See walk number 7, p. 53 and Don't Miss p. 79.

Scuola Grande di San Rocco and Santa Maria dei Frari basilica

These two magnificent buildings are home to a number of masterpieces by Tiziano, Canova and Bellini. The area is also ideal for taking romantic walks, far from the touristic crowds.

See walk number 10, pp. 58-59 and Don't Miss p. 80.

Ca' Rezzonico

From its magnificent ballroom to its library and its so-called "room of the Nuptial Allegory," the Ca' Rezzonico is full of wonderful paintings and exquisite decorations.

See walk number 8, p. 55 and Don't Miss p. 81.

Ponte di Rialto

After the Accademia bridge and the Bridge of Sighs, you must see the third of Venice's most famous bridges: the Rialto and its busy shopping area.

See walk number 9, p. 56 and Don't Miss p. 82.

San Giovanni e Paolo basilica

This church is also known as "San Zanipolo." After having admired this Gothic monument's impressive proportions, one can also see the magnificent statue of Bartholomeo Colleoni, the mercenary, which stands in front of the church.

See walk number 12, p. 63 and Don't Miss p. 83.

1

Piazza San Marco

Massive monuments, luxury stores on every side, crowds mingling with flocks of pigeons and the endless clicking of cameras all make this "Europe's finest drawing-room," as Napoleon once described it. You can visit this display of splendor time and time again and never tire of it. In the early dawn light, at sunset or by night, the Piazza San Marco is more fascinating than ever.

❶ Piazza San Marco★★★

See Don't Miss p. 72.

The vast St Mark's Square, the most famous attraction in Venice, is the only square in the city to be graced with the title *piazza*, so called because the Venetians wanted to mark its importance in the city compared to the other *campi*.

❷ Basilica di San Marco★★★

☎ 041 522 52 05
(*Pala d'Oro* and Treasury)
Mon.-Sat. 9.30am-5pm,
Sun. 2-4pm
Entrance charge for *galleria*
See Don't Miss p. 73.

The *chiesa d'oro* (golden church), squat and glittering with some 4,800 sq. yd of mosaics, dates from the 11th century. Among the countless art objects it contains is the *Pala d'Oro*, a gold altarpiece encrusted with 80 enamels and 3,000 precious stones. Don't miss the climb up to the gallery, where you can see the square from between the hooves of San Marco's famous horses (copies, but still impressive).

❸ Campanile★★

☎ 041 522 40 64
Every day 9.30am-7pm (9pm or 10pm in summer). Charge for elevator.

The campanile collapsed without warning in 1912,

but luckily the only victim was a cat, and it was soon rebuilt exactly as before. The view of Venice from the top is a must.

❹ Palazzo Ducale★★★

☎ 041 271 59 11
Nov.1 -Mar. 31,
Every day 9am-5pm;
Apr. 1-Oct. 31, 9am-7pm
Entrance charge (ticket office closes 1h earlier).
See Don't Miss p. 74.

In this marvel of Gothic architecture (1340–1424), each room is more beautiful than the last. Some are decorated by Veronese, others by Tintoretto, who created the largest oil painting in the world for the Grand Council Chamber, *Vision of Paradise*, 22m by 7m (72ft by 23ft).

❺ Torre dell'Orologio★★

☎ 041 271 59 11
Restoration will be completed soon. Ask for more information.

The clock tower is decorated with the signs of the zodiac and the lion of St Mark, and crowned with two statues of Moors who strike the hours on a large bell.

❻ Piazzetta★★

With its gondolas moored at the quayside and the island of San Giorgio Maggiore in the distance, this "little square" presents one of the most photogenic landscapes in Venice. The two columns, surmounted by a winged lion, the symbol of St Mark, and by St Theodore, the first patron saint of the city, were brought back from the Orient.

❼ Quadri★★

Piazza San Marco, 120
☎ 041 522 21 05
Every day 9.30am-midnight.

The indispensable counterpart to Florian (opened in 1775), with decor only slightly less chic and delightful, an equally hushed atmosphere and comparably high prices. The price of drinks inevitably goes up when the orchestras are playing, competing with each other across the piazza.

❽ FLORIAN★★★

This café opened in 1720 and is a real gem. It was once the meeting place of artists and poets, and boasts many famous people among its past clientele. Come back time and again to sample the pastries and get to know every part of it. You'll get a charming welcome, too.

Piazza San Marco, 56-59; ☎ 041 520 56 41 www.caffeflorian.com; every day except Wed. in winter, 10am-midnight.

2

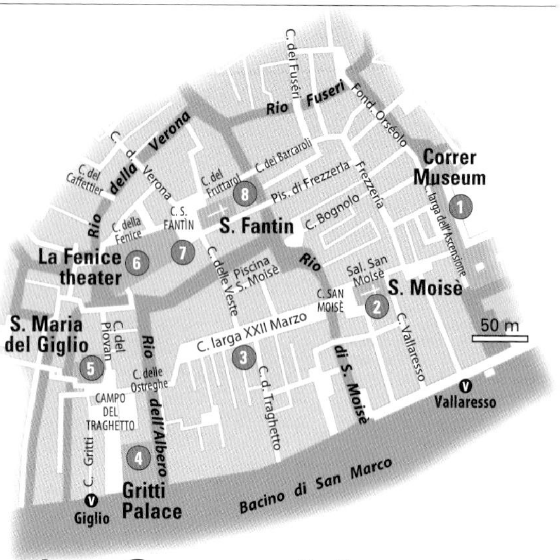

From the Correr Museum
to La Fenice

In a district studded with churches and crisscrossed by canals or quiet *campi* you can discover most of the smartest stores, and some of the best antique dealers and art galleries in Venice.

❶ Correr Museum★★★

Piazza San Marco, 52
entrance via Ala Napoleonica
☎ 041 240 52 11
Every day 9am-5pm in winter, until 7pm in summer. Entrance charge.

This huge and beautiful museum (allow half a day for a visit) relates the great times of the history of Venice. From the entrance admire the sculptures by Canova. The ticket also enables you to visit the Archaeological Museum and the rooms of the Marciana National Library, inside the Correr Museum. As for the art gallery, it possesses a fine collection of paintings, not only Venetian ones. As well as Bellinis, there's a sublime *Pietà* by Antonello da Messina that's worth a close study.

❷ Church of San Moisè★

Campo San Moisè
☎ 041 528 58 40
Every day 9-12am, 3.30-7pm.

The Venetians must have been short of saints to venerate when they canonized Moses and dedicated this church to him in the 17th century. This example of unbridled Baroque stands next to the appalling façade of the Bauer-Grünwald hotel.

❸ La calle larga XXII Marzo

The smartest street in Venice and home to the great names

in fashion, leather goods and high-quality souvenirs. Visitors never seem to tire of walking up and down here, and in its extension, the Salizzada San Moisè and the little Calle Vallaresso. The buildings are impressive, and even the banks resemble grand monuments.

❹ Gritti Palace Hotel★★

Campo Santa Maria del Giglio, 2467
☎ 041 794 611
Ⓕ 041 520 09 42.

With its 17th-century furniture, Persian carpets, waterside restaurant and view of the Grand Canal, the Gritti is one of the top ten hotels in the world. The prices are astronomical, of course, but money isn't usually an issue if you come to stay at the Gritti!

❺ Church of Santa Maria del Giglio and its campo★

☎ 041 275 04 62
Mon.-Sat. 10am-5pm, Sun. 1-5pm; closed Sun. in Aug. Entrance charge.

The *campo* dominated by Santa Maria del Giglio (the

Church of the Lily) is the gondoliers' headquarters. In the evening, it echoes to serenades performed by the men in straw boaters. Come here to dream of eternal Venice.

❼ Al Teatro restaurant★

Campo San Fantin, 1916
☎ 041 522 10 52
Every day except Mon., 12am-3.30pm, 6.30-8.30pm.

One of the two obligatory places to go after a performance at La Fenice (the other is Antico Martini, see p. 90), serving some of the best cuisine in Venice. Prices are high, as you might expect. Cigarettes – usually only sold in tobacco shops – are also on sale here.

❽ Church of San Fantin★

Campo San Fantin
Every day 7.30am-noon and 4-7pm.

Facing La Fenice, this magnificent white stone Renaissance building is the joint creation of two of Venice's best architects, Scarpagnigno and Sansovino, who built the dome resting on four impressive Corinthian columns. The nearby *scuola* houses thirteen works by the painter Palma the Younger.

❻ LA FENICE THEATER★★★

Farinelli's *Idomeneus*, Rossini's *Tancred*, Verdi's *Rigoletto* or *Traviata* and so many other operas were born here, in La Fenice. Built in 1792 the theater burned down in 1836 for the first time, then again in January 1996. Venice decided it should come to life again *com'era e dov'era*, "as it used to be and where it was." The reconstruction lasted for eight years. Today, the love of the Venetians for their theater has not changed. La Fenice is the same, or nearly the same.

Campo San Fantin, 2549; ☎ 041 241 80 33
www.teatrolafenice.it
Visits possible during the day: Information at the ticket office; Mon.-Sat. 8.30am-6.30pm.

3

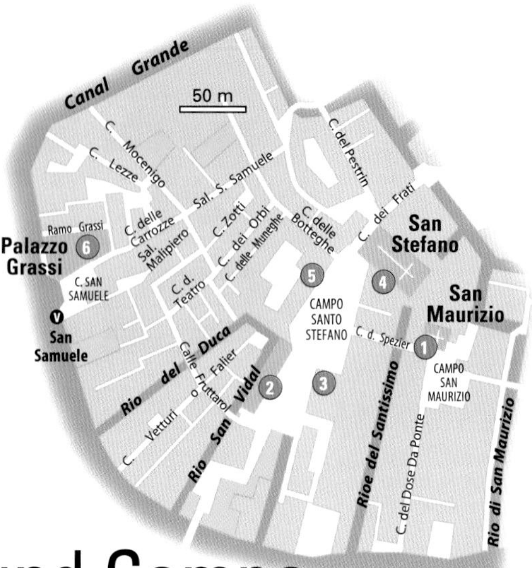

Around Campo San Stefano

In the peaceful atmosphere, spacious squares stretch lazily in the sunshine, surrounded by alleyways and little humpbacked bridges; a stroll is always delightful. Out of season, the mist floats above the canals, adding mystery and melancholy to the beautiful surroundings.

❶ Campo San Maurizio★

The Church of San Maurizio (rebuilt in the 19th century)

and the Lombardesque façade of the Scuola degli Albanesi (16th century) stand in a quiet little *campo* that will leave you with fond memories. The Palazzo Bellavite is also worth a look, although it's lost the Veronese frescoes with which it was once decorated. Venice's secondhand market is held in this charming setting several times a year.

❷ The palaces of Campo San Stefano★

Closed to the public.

The Campo San Stefano used to be covered with grass, and was used for bullfights

until the early 19th century. Three of the most powerful Venetian families chose this oddly shaped esplanade to build a series of sumptuous palaces – the Loredans in the

16th century, the Morosinis in the 17th century and the Pisanis in the 18th century.

❸ Fiorellashop★

Campo San Stefano, 2806, San Marco
☎ 041 520 92 28
Every day except Sun. 10am-7pm (sometimes closed 1-3pm).

A strange-looking collection of velvet jackets is displayed on hermaphrodite *doges* wearing high heels.

This imaginative store window recalls the stylist Fiorella Mancini, a key figure in the Carnival.

❹ Church of San Stefano★

Campo San Stefano
☎ 041 522 50 61
Every day 8am-7pm.

Flanked by a bell tower that leans at an alarming angle, the church is entered via a remarkable Flamboyant Gothic portal. You'll find some paintings worth viewing by some of the greatest artists (Vivarini, Palma the Elder and Tintoretto) housed in the nave and sacristy.

❺ San Stefano ice cream parlor★

Campo San Stefano, 2962, San Marco
☎ 041 522 55 76
Every day 10am-midnight in season, until 8.30pm out of season; closed Nov.-Dec.and Tue. out of season.

The home of traditional Venetian ice cream. Don't miss it – it's an institution.

❻ Palazzo Grassi★★

Campo San Samuele, 3231, San Marco
☎ 041 523 16 80
Every day 10am-7pm during exhibitions
See Don't Miss p. 75.

This gigantic palace, built by the Grassi family in 1730, was the last to be built along the Grand Canal. The building, which was sinking into the lagoon, was restored in 1986. The car manufacturer, Fiat, owns the walls and sponsors outstanding annual exhibitions (including Marcel Duchamp, Henry Moore and Giambattista Tiepolo). The café is run by Harry's Bar (see p. 96), a sure sign of quality, so you can feel confident about eating there.

SECONDHAND MARKET IN CAMPO SAN MAURIZIO

If you love old objects but despair at the astronomical prices asked by Venetian antique dealers for the smallest knickknack, there's only one solution: go to the market on the San Maurizio campo, generally held at Easter, also during the 3rd weekend in September and the weekend just before Christmas. Ask at the tourist information center or look in the *Bussola* leaflet. When making a deal, never lose sight of the fact that the Serenissima still remembers a time when it traded with the Orient, so expect some hard bargaining.

4

From Fortuny Museum to Campo San Luca

Antiques shops looking like small museums and craft shops can be found next to bakeries, local cafés and all sorts of little shops you might fall in love with. And, if you want to get away from the crowds, or find some romantic solitude, climb up to the Palazzo Contarini del Bovolo.

❶ Museo Fortuny★★

Palazzo Pesaro degli Orfei, 3780, San Marco
☎ 041 520 09 95;
Open only during exhibitions
Tue.-Sun. 10am-5.30pm.

This museum, located inside the Gothic walls of the splendid Pesaro Palace (15th century), presents an interesting collection of fabrics to which the Andalusian Mariano Fortuny y Madrazo (1871–1949) gave his name (see p. 16). You can find out all about his work here and see a wealth of marvelous and unusual scarves and dresses.

❷ Palazzo Corner-Spinelli★★

☎ 041 258 44 11
Mon.-Fri. 8.30-12.30am, 3.30-7.30pm.

The house of Rubelli – one of the great names of Venetian fabrics (see p. 110) – needed a head office to match its prestige, and since moving into this fine palace, it has one. The palace itself was built between 1490 and 1510. However, its purpose hasn't

changed. Its former owners, the Spinellis, were themselves merchants who grew rich on the silk trade.

❸ Campo Sant'Angelo★

This aristocratic square lined with palaces is a pleasant place to rest before embarking on a shopping expedition in the neighboring *calle*. The church of San Michele (the archangel), who gave his name to the *campo*, has disappeared. All that remains is a little oratory adorned with a graceful bell tower. The nearby canal and its pretty bridge are quite charming.

❹ Acqua Pazza restaurant

Campo Sant'Angelo, 3808-3810, San Marco
☎ 041 277 06 88
Reservation essential. Closed Mon.

Fine Italian cuisine is celebrated daily in this fish restaurant which has become the ultimate reference for Venetians in terms of sea food (budget for €50 per person). Run by a Neapolitan, the restaurant serves traditional dishes from the Amalfi coast. Try the *laganelle alla scoglio*, the *cannerozzi con cozze e scampi* and in the warm season ask for a table on their lovely terrace.

❻ Campo Manin★

The center of Venice also has some 20th-century monuments, such as the *Cassa di Risparmio* (Savings Bank) built in the *campo* in 1968. While it would be a little misleading to say that the building has been a complete success, it does demonstrate that Venice isn't just a museum city as is too often stated. The vast quadrilateral of the Campo Manin proudly bears the name of the Venetian revolutionary who drove out the Austrians and proclaimed the Republic in 1848.

❼ Campo San Luca★★

Venetians and tourists alike gather on this friendly and lively *campo* where a marble plinth marks the center of town. You will enjoy stopping for a welcome ice cream before diving into the very narrow calle dei Fabbri, full of busy stores, or stepping across the Rialto Bridge.

❺ PALAZZO CONTARINI DEL BOVOLO★★

Renaissance, Gothic or Byzantine – it would take a genius to label this strange 15th-century palace lying off the beaten tourist track, just by Campo Manin. The fact remains that its name (*bovolo* means spiral staircase in the Venetian dialect) is entirely fitting and it's impossible to confuse it with any other palace in the city. Its quiet little courtyard and lacy openwork staircase are quite irresistible. Unfortunately, only the staircase is open to the public.

Corte Contarini del Bovolo; ☎ 041 270 24 64
Apr.-Oct., Every day 10am-6pm; Entrance charge.

5

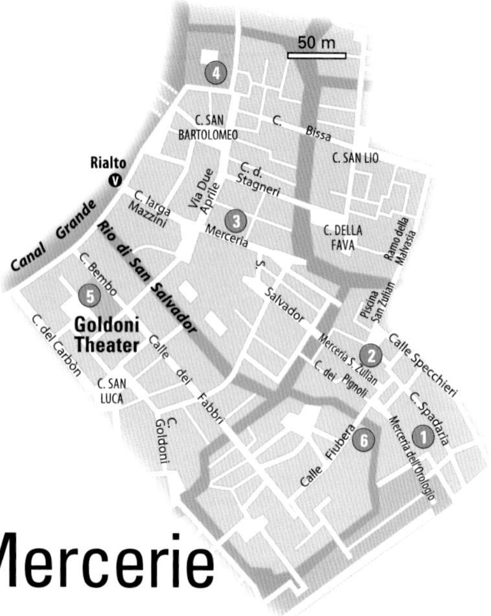

The Mercerie

Just behind Piazza San Marco, there is an open-air shopping mall. Add a few bottlenecks and a succession of bridges and tempting shopwindows to slow down the crowds, and you have the Mercerie. Once the home of sellers of fabric, it's still the liveliest place in the city today.

❶ Merceria dell'Orologio★

The Merceria dell'Orologio starts, as its name suggests, under the clock tower of Piazza San Marco (Torre dell'Orologio, see p. 41). The stores that line this narrow *calle* are in a different league to those of the *piazza*. Exorbitant jewelry stores, expensive shoe stores and a few shops offering unusual junk compete with *trattorie* for undemanding tourists.

❷ Merceria San Zulian★★

If you get tired of the hustle and bustle of the Mercerie, leave the jostling crowds behind you and escape to Campo San Zulian. It will seem surprisingly calm and village-like in comparison. The maze of dark alleyways behind the church, in the direction of Santa Maria Formosa (see p. 63), is packed with food stores. Porters shouting *attenzione!* at the passers-by and housewives armed with shopping baskets mingle happily with the crowds of tourists.

❸ Merceria and Church of San Salvador★

Church open every day 9.30am-5.30pm.

The Baroque façade of the Church of San Salvador conceals many marvels, including some paintings

by Titian and the beautiful *Cena in Emaus* by Bellini. This painting is a copy, but a period one at least. The same succession of stores runs the length of the Merceria San Salvador. Some are worth stopping at, others less so. Once you have established which ones are the quality stores, and which sell bland "touristy" items, you are in for a good time.

❹ Fondaco dei Tedeschi★★

San Marco, 5554
☎ 041 271 72 36
Mon.-Sat. 8.30am-6.30pm.

This is the main post office of Venice. Buying stamps or phoning from within the walls of this venerable *fondaco* (15th century), which was originally decorated with frescoes by Giorgione and Titian (the ones that could be saved are now at the Ca' d'Oro, see p. 65), is actually quite exciting. Especially when you know that the building was once the headquarters of the German merchants (the *Tedeschi*) who traded with the Serenissima.

❺ Antica Carbonera restaurant★★

Calle Bembo, 4648
☎ 041 522 54 79
Every day except Thu. and Fri.; lunchtime 12-3pm and evening 7-10pm.

A welcome with a smile, an elegant but unpretentious setting (it's rather like being on a boat), and some of the best value for money in the vicinity of Piazza San Marco. Choose spaghetti *alle vongole* (with clams) and a very rare steak washed down with a good Venetian wine, and you can't fail to be content.

❻ VALESE FOUNDRY SHOP★★

Since 1918, the name Alberto Valese has been the last word in the art of casting *alla veneziana*. The shop is entirely devoted to bronze, tin, copper and cast iron and is overflowing with lamps, door knockers and key rings. Here you can buy one of the fifty types of little horses that adorn the sides of gondolas, which are still made the traditional way in molds filled with sand from the Forest of Fontainebleau. The foundry (Fondamenta Madonna dell'Orto, 3535 Cannaregio ☎ 041 72 02 34) can be visited by appointment.

Calle Fiubera, 793
San Marco
☎ 041 522 72 82
Every day except Sun. 10.30am-12.30pm and 3-7pm outside season, 10.30am-7pm in season.

6

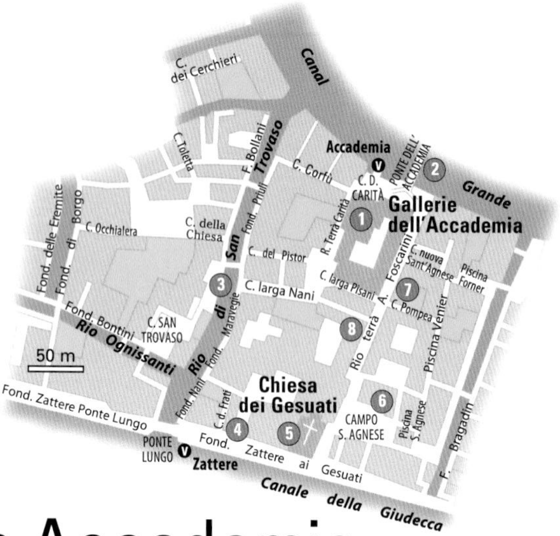

The Accademia quarter

Silence reigns along the tranquil *rio*. The occasional steamer passes along the Canale della Giudecca, and the air carries the scent of the sea. Toward San Trovaso, in the shade of a Palladian church, craftsmen still patiently and meticulously construct gondolas with as little regard for the passage of time as the district itself.

❶ Accademia gallery★★★

Campo della Carità
☎ 041 522 22 47
Tue.-Sun. 8.15am-7.15pm, Mon. 8.15am-2pm; Entrance charge (ticket office closes 45 minutes earlier)
See Don't Miss p. 76.

Venice's largest museum possesses an amazing number of masterpieces. It's just a pity the lighting's so bad. Avoid late afternoons in winter. Among the

paintings you simply mustn't miss are *Miracle of the True Cross at San Lorenzo* by Bellini, the *Legend of St Ursula* by Carpaccio, the *Tempesta* by Giorgione, the *Pietà* by Titian, the *Miracle of St Mark* by Tintoretto, *Supper in the House of Levi* by Veronese, and a number of Tiepolos, Guardis and Longhis.

❷ Ponte dell'Accademia★

This iron bridge was built by the Austrians in 1854, then demolished under Mussolini before being rebuilt in its original form in 1985. It offers a fine view of the Grand Canal and its succession of palaces dominated by the silhouette of the Church of Santa Maria della Salute.

❸ Campo Sant'Agnese★

Church closed to the public.

A quiet *campo* that has kept its medieval face intact. For a change, nobody thought it necessary to give the old Church of Sant'Agnese (12th to 13th century) a Baroque makeover. It's the ideal place to stop for a few moments' quiet contemplation.

❺ Church of Gesuati★

Fondamenta delle Zattere
☎ 041 275 04 62
Every day 9am-5pm, Sun. 1-5pm
Entrance charge.

The façade of the old Jesuit church (18th century) is the counterpart of the large Palladian buildings on the other side of the Canale della Giudecca (see p. 66). The interior conceals a stunning trompe l'œil ceiling by Tiepolo (*Apotheosis of St Dominic*).

❻ Zattere ai Gesuati★★★

The wide banks of the canal (literally "pontoons") provide one of the Venetians' favorite places to walk – a popular spot for sunbathing, jogging, eating ice cream or going for a drink.

❼ Agli Alboretti restaurant★★

Rio terrà A. Foscarini, 882-884, Dorsoduro
☎ 041 523 00 58
Every day except Wed. and Thu.; 12.30-2.30pm and 7.30-10.30pm; closed Jan. and Aug.

A small family hotel (reservations essential) a stone's throw from the Accademia. It's quiet and friendly, like the district itself. In the morning you can have breakfast outside in the shady garden, and the excellent restaurant is one of the best in the square.

❽ La Rivista★★★

Dorsoduro, 979/A
☎ 041 240 14 25
Every day except Mon. 12-3pm and 7-11pm; bar service 3-7pm.

Just behind the Accademia, this fashionable restaurant has built its reputation on the quality of its ingredients and on the originality of its recipes such as its pasta with cabbage and foie gras, or grilled eels with fennel and artichokes. A gourmet address (discovery menu for €58.50).

❹ AROUND SAN TROVASO★★★

The wooden shacks of the Squero San Trovaso (closed to the public), one of the oldest gondola yards in the city, lie at the junction of two canals. The skiffs that are the very soul of Venice are still made here in accordance with age-old tradition. The Palladian church (open every day except Sun. 8-11am and 3-6pm; ☎ 041 522 21 33) dedicated to St Gervase and St Protase (*Trovaso* is the contraction of Gervasio and Protasio) dominates this charming place.

See Don't Miss p. 77.

7

The Dorsoduro headland

Overlooked by the triumphant dome of the Della Salute church, this part of the Dorsoduro (the "hard back" or "spine") is an ideal place to rest from the bustle of San Marco Square and get some fresh air. In these quiet *calle*, you will find some art galleries, among which the inescapable Guggenheim Foundation. Don't miss the peaceful *zattere*, along the Giudecca Canal, spectacularly lit up at night.

❶ Peggy Guggenheim Foundation★★★

Palazzo Ca' Venier dei Leoni, Dorsoduro, 701

☎ 041 240 55 11
www.guggenheim-venice.it
Foundation and Museum Shop, every day except Tue. 10am-6pm. Entrance charge.
See Don't Miss p. 78.

The wife of Max Ernst had two passions: her dogs and art. All the modern art movements are represented here, from Picasso and Miró to Pollock, without forgetting the sculptures of Brancusi and Marini which are exhibited on the terrace facing the Grand Canal. There are also a good bookstore and temporary exhibitions.

❷ Palazzo Dario★★

Closed to the public.
This delightful palace on the Grand Canal, with a

façade resembling a jewelry box, is more like the work of a sculptor or painter than that of an architect. It was once the residence of Giovanni Dario, who took on the perilous role of ambassador of Venice to the Ottoman Empire in the late 15th century

❸ Church of San Gregorio★

Closed to the public.
People actually work in this beautiful 15th-century church. It's where most of Venice's works of art are sent when they are in need of restoration. It goes without saying, therefore, that the workshops are always busy.

❺ Dogana di Mara and Punta della Dogana★★

If you're looking for a pleasant stroll, follow the Punta della Dogana (customs point) around under the arcades of the old 17th-century Dogana di Mara (maritime customs house). It's not difficult to picture the ships that once docked here, and the illustrious artists who fell in love with the place, including Canaletto, Turner and Monet.

❻ Zattere ai Saloni and al Santo Spirito★

Church: Sun. 8am-12pm and 3-6pm.
Walk along opposite the island of the Giudecca, past the old salt warehouses, the Church of Santo Spirito and a number of very tempting terraces. Music lovers shouldn't miss taking a look at the Ospedale degli Incurabili (closed to the public), once reserved for syphilitics, before being turned into a boarding school for gifted young musicians.

❼ Marina e Susanna Sent

San Vio, 669-670/A,
☎ 041 520 81 36
Every day 10am-6pm.

A boutique gallery presenting the Sent sisters' creations: beautiful glass pearl jewelry (around €32), merino wool scarves, vases and other objects in glass. Such is the excellence of their craftsmanship that their work is also exhibited in a number of the town's museums, such as the Museo dell'Arte Vetraria in Murano.

❹ CHURCH OF SANTA MARIA DELLA SALUTE★★★

Venice erected this large rotunda in 1630 to thank the Virgin for ending the terrible plague epidemic which had raged through the city. The Festival of the Salute (see p. 21) still dutifully commemorates the event. The architect of this masterly example of Baroque art, Baldassare Longhena, didn't skimp on the statues or pinnacle turrets, or on the size of the dome either. Once inside, you feel very small, but the overall effect is stunning.

Campo della Salute, ☎ 041 274 39 11
Every day 9am-12pm and 3-6pm;
organ concerts some days.
See Don't Miss p. 79.

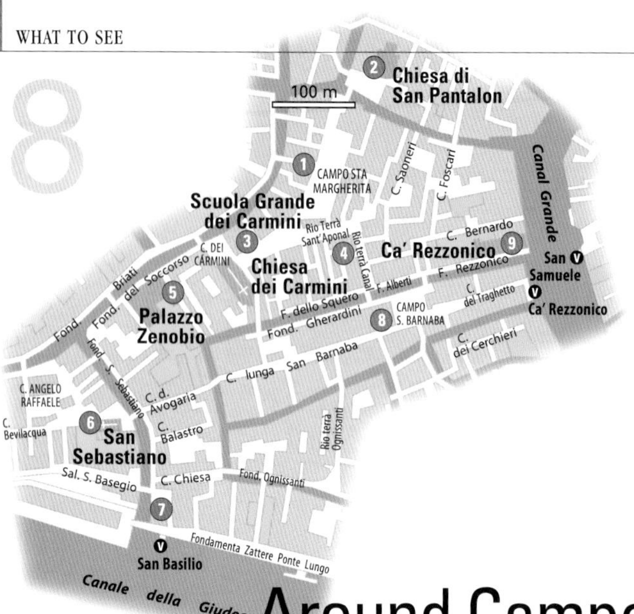

Around Campo Santa Margherita

The terraces of the Campo Santa Margherita are the domain of students: the university and several higher education establishments are just a stone's throw away. In the evening, the area becomes one of the "in" places to go for a drink or listen to a concert. During the day, you can discover a peaceful and very attractive village-like atmosphere.

❶ Campo Santa Margherita★

A charming little square with cafés and terraces, where one can rest in the shade. There are boutiques, a market on certain days and elegant houses from the 14th and 15th centuries.

❷ Church of San Pantalon★★

Mon.-Sat. 8-10am, 4-6pm.

For those who are interested in trompe l'oeil frescoes, the ceiling of nearby San Pantalon is a must.This work of art will leave you stunned when you realize that it is not a fresco but a 900²m (9700²ft) canvas!

❷ Campo San Barnaba★

Church: irregular opening hours.

A real treat. This is the epitomy of Venice – a simple *campo* lined with a few cafés, dominated as you'd expect by a church flanked by a magnificent 14th-century bell tower. From here a quiet *fondamenta* runs alongside a *rio*, where picturesque truck farmers' boats are moored.

❸ Church of S. M. del Carmelo and la Scuola Grande dei Carmini★★

Campo dei Carmini
Scuola: ☎ 041 528 94 20
Mon.-Sat. 9am-6pm, Sun. and holidays 9am-4pm
Church: ☎ 041 522 65 53
Mon.-Sat. 7.30am-12pm and 2.30-7pm, Sun. during services.

If the church is an interesting example of Renaissance architecture, the *scuola* is a curiosity of the first order – the entire decoration of the upper floor was entrusted to Tiepolo, who finished the work in ten years, between 1739 and 1749.

❺ Palazzo Zenobio★★

Collegio Armeno
Fondamenta del soccorso, 2596
☎ 041 522 87 70
Visits possible by appointment.

With its Baroque façade, the late 17th-century Palazzo Zenobio may at first seem incongruous under the Venetian sky. The interior is a marvel of trompe l'œil decoration, a festival of stucco, antique furniture, gilded frames and Venetian mirrors.

❻ Church of San Sebastiano★★★

Campo San Sebastiano
☎ 041 275 04 62
Mon.-Sat. 10am-5pm, Sun. 1-5pm
Entrance charge.

This church, hidden behind a modest exterior, conceals one of the most dazzling interiors that Veronese ever painted for the Serenissima. Everything, from the ceiling with its trompe l'œil frescoes to the altarpieces, and even the organ under which the artist is buried, was executed by Paolo Caliari, otherwise known as Veronese.

❹ CA' REZZONICO★★★

The Venetian palaces can be frustrating. You can only imagine interiors that are as magnificent, opulent and unique as their exteriors, as their doors are often closed. This venerable building (18th century), with its sublime interior decoration (marble, trompe l'œil and painted ceilings), will leave you speechless with admiration and have you fantasizing about the riches hidden inside the city's other palaces. The museum collection is devoted exclusively to Venetian painting of the Enlightenment, and will leave you with a lasting impression if you like the work of Canaletto, Tiepolo and Longhi.

Fondamenta Rezzonico, 3136, ☎ 041 241 01 00
Every day except Tue. 10am-6pm
Entrance charge (ticket office closes at 5pm).

❼ L'Incontro restaurant★

Rio terrà Canal (Ponte dei Pugni)
Campo S. Margherita, 3062/A
☎ 041 522 24 04
Every day except Mon. and Tue.; 12.30-2.30pm and 7.30pm-10.30pm.

An original restaurant just behind the Campo Santa Margherita where you can sample a cuisine you may not have tried before – Sardinian. The terrace is an ideal spot for watching the lively scene in the *campo* (around €25–€30).

❽ Trattoria San Basilio★

Fondamenta Zattere, 1516
☎ 041 521 00 28
Every day except Sun. 12.30-3pm and 7-9.30pm.

Looking onto the water lapping gently by the *vaporetto* stop of San Basilio, this unpretentious *trattoria* offers a menu of pasta and simple salads offering good value for money, which is quite rare on the *zattere*.

9

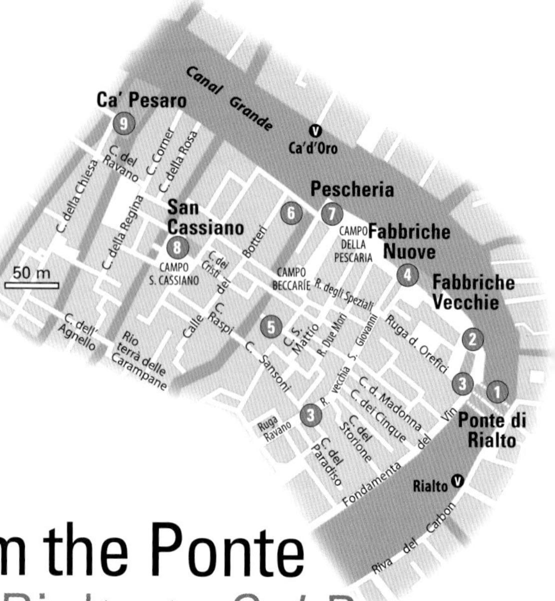

From the Ponte di Rialto to Ca' Pesaro

The Ca' Pesaro, less well known to the general public than the Guggenheim, also has rare works to display when it comes to modern art. It is very close to the famous Rialto Bridge, where for centuries the entire population of Venice has come to do its shopping in a very Mediterranean atmosphere.

❶ Ponte di Rialto★★★

See Don't Miss p. 82.

Without the Rialto Bridge, the main link beween the two banks of Venice's Grand Canal, it wouldn't be the city it is today. Built of stone in the late 16th century, the "Rialto" remained the only bridge over the Grand Canal until the 19th century. It was difficult to build and progress was slow. Not only did it rest on unstable ground, but its height was considered an amazing feat for the time (7.5m/25ft, to allow the galleys to pass underneath). As in Florence, gold- and silversmiths set up shop on it, and several of the portico shops still carry on the tradition.

❷ Botteghe della solidarietà★★

S. Marco, 5164, Rialto
☎ 041 522 75 45
Every day 9.30am-8pm.

Just next to the Rialto, an address for those who like the flavor of authenticity. You'll find various local products such as suede leather bags, toys and various bio food preparations. Try the exquisite capers and artichokes olive oil paste. You will also find Indonesian jewelry and Indian musical instruments.

❸ La Ruga degli Orefici and la Ruga Vecchia★

The Street of the Goldsmiths (Ruga degli Orefici or degli Oresi) and the "Old Street" (Ruga Vecchia) are like the shopping streets in a village. They're extremely lively when the market's in full swing, between 11am and noon. More jewelry stores can be

found under the arcades of the gallery parallel to the Ruga degli Orefici.

❹ Fabbriche Vecchie e Nuove★

Closed to the public.

The arcaded buildings that once housed the administration of trade, and of navigation and supplies, have stood beside the Grand Canal since the 16th century. Built respectively by Scarpagnino and Sansovino, they today house the court of justice.

❺ Cantina Do Mori★

S. Polo, 401, Rialto
☎ 041 522 54 01
Mon.-Sat. 8.30am-8.30pm.

One of Venice's most famous *bacari*, Cantino Do Mori is the ideal place to taste all kinds of regional wines while eating cod *baccalà*, artichoke *crostini* or various types of sandwich.

❻ Trattoria Poste Vecie★

Campo della Pescaria, 1608
☎ 041 72 18 22
Every day except Tue. 7-10.30pm.

This trattoria near the fish market, a stone's throw from the Grand Canal, is said to be the oldest in Venice. Whether this is true or not, the *insalata di cape sante* (scallop salad) is excellent, as are the other fish dishes. There's a fine wine list, too.

❼ Pescheria★

Market every morning 8am-noon except Sun. and Mon.

This is Venice's fish market, where Venetian housewives come to shop after their obligatory trip to the Erberia fruit and vegetable market (every day except Sun. 8am-noon).

❽ Church of San Cassiano and its campo★

Campo San Cassiano
Tue.-Sat. 9am-noon.

The church itself is a patchwork of styles and houses an unusual *Crucifixion* by Tintoretto. But the real charm of the place lies elsewhere, in the quiet *campo* bordered by the Rio Cassiano.

❾ CA' PESARO★★

Designed by Longhena in the late 17th century, this palace houses works that were bought at the first Venice Biennales (see pp. 20–21).The collectioin features some real treasures including a very fine Klimt. Whatever happens, don't miss the collection of Japanese art in the Oriental museum.

Fondamenta Mocenigo, Santa Croce
Galleria d'Arte moderna and Museo d'Arte orientale
☎ 041 524 11 73
10am-6pm Apr.-Oct., 5pm out of season; closed Mon.; Entrance charge. Ticket office closes one hour earlier.

10

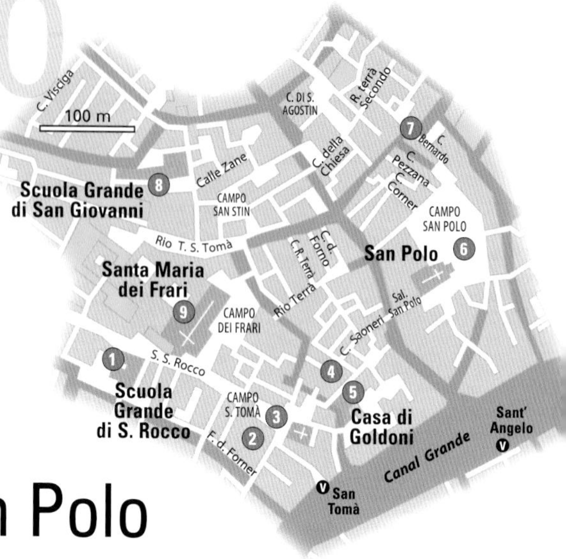

San Polo

Casa di Goldoni, the exceptional Basilica dei Frari, where Monteverdi and Titian were laid to rest, the Scuola di San Rocco, decorated by Tintoretto and the district of Santa Maria dei Frari – what a heritage! And don't forget a few bars where you can start your evening.

❶ Scuola Grande di San Rocco★★★

Campo San Rocco
Scuola : Every day Apr.-Oct. 9am-5.30pm, Nov.-Mar. 10am-4pm
☎ 041 523 48 64
Entrance charge (ticket office closes 30 mins earlier)
Church: Every day 7.30am-12.30pm (2-4pm weekends in winter)
☎ 041 523 48 64
See Don't Miss p. 80.

Imagine two floors entirely covered in paintings by Tintoretto and you'll have some idea of how marvelous this is – it's an absolute must. Fans of Jacopo Robusti can't afford to miss the Renaissance church opposite.

❷ Michele Cigogna★★

Campo San Tomà, 2867
☎ / Ⓕ 041 522 76 78
Mon.-Fri. 9am-12.30pm, 3.30-6pm.

A well-established restorer and manufacturer of traditional furniture and

paintings, with a workshop dating from the 19th century. The little painted wooden caskets in the shopwindow are tempting but pricey, as are the gilded frames. Michele Cigogna also paints pictures to order.

3 Campo San Tomà★★

Campo San Tomà
Church closed to public.

A little square dominated by an 18th-century church, sober in style. Opposite is the old shoemakers' *scuola* with its popular low-relief ornate portal. The area is very popular on account of the two "big names" of Venetian chic, the jeweler Sfriso (see p. 109) and the boutique belonging to Michele Cigogna.

4 Bar ai Nomboli★

Calle dei Nomboli, 2717/C
☎ 041 523 09 95
Every day except Sun. 7am-9pm; closed Sat.-Sun. in winter.

It's well worth stopping in this discreet little bar next to San Tomà, if only to taste their delicious panini sandwiches at very reasonable prices. An example of one surprising combination (among many others): shrimp, salad and artichokes. Value for money!

5 Casa di Goldoni★

Palazzo Centani
Calle dei Nomboli, 2794
☎ 041 244 03 17
Every day except Sun. 10am-5pm. Entrance charge. Ticket office closed 30 mins earlier.

Lodged inside a Gothic Palace, the playwright Carlo Goldoni's birthplace became a museum in 1931.

6 Campo and church of San Polo★

☎ 041 275 04 62
Church: Mon.-Sat. 10am-5pm, Sun. 1-5pm
Entrance charge.

This *campo* comes to life during the Carnival and the Mostra Film festival, when it is transformed into an open-air movie theater. If you feel like a drink, there are several cafés, and a fountain in perfect working order (rare in Venice). The church, sober in style, is home to 14 paintings by Tiepolo and to works by Tintoretto and Veronese.

7 Da Fiore restaurant ★★

Calle del Scateler, 2202
☎ 041 72 13 08
Tue.-Sat. 12.30-2.30pm and 7-10pm.
Closed Dec. 25-Jan 15.

Very expensive and very good, this fish restaurant has become a Venetian institution.

8 Scuola Grande di San Giovanni★★

Campiello de la Scuola
☎ 041 71 82 34
Visits by appointment.

Worth a visit just for the magnificent marble portal by Pietro Lombardo (*c.*1480) embossed with an eagle, the symbol of John the Baptist.

9 BASILICA DI SANTA MARIA DEI FRARI★★★

Grandiose, magnificent, gigantic, extraordinary: Words fail to accurately describe this church erected by the Franciscans between 1340 and 1443. With this monument, Venetian Gothic reached a level of perfection never equaled since. A fine example of Venetian Gothic architecture at its peak, the dazzling interior houses an amazing collection of works of art that are among the best ever produced in Venice. It's difficult to know where to look first – at the brilliant *Assumption* by Titian (on the high altar), dubbed the most beautiful painting in the world, the mellow Bellini (in the sacristy) or the strange pyramidal tomb by Canova.

Campo dei Frari,
☎ 041 275 04 62
Mon.-Sat. 9am-6pm, Sun. 1-6pm; Entrance charge
See Don't Miss p. 80.

11

Around San Zaccaria

Just next to the Piazza San Marco, on the quay dedicated to Dalmatia (Schiavonia), façades and palaces look out onto one of the most beautiful views in the world. Only a handful of tourists bother to go on any further, and a good thing, too. Peace and quiet are vital to appreciate the important sights concealed behind the village atmosphere of this part of the Sestiere of Castello, that Canaletto immortalized in his paintings.

❶ Ponte dei Sospiri★★

The famous Bridge of Sighs (1614) was used to link the prison cells to the tribunal of the Doges' Palace. The prisoners used to walk across it sighing – particularly at the time of the Inquisition – hence its name. The classic view from the Ponte della Paglia, on the side of the ducal palace, is definitely the best but often teeming with people! So don't hesitate to go and admire it from the other side or at less crowded times.

❷ Danieli Palace★★

Riva degli Schiavoni, 4196
☎ 041 522 64 80.

This dream of a hotel, with its chandeliers, antique furniture and thick carpets isn't cheap, but at least you'll be able to say you've walked in the footsteps of the great,

from Balzac and de Musset to George Sand and Wagner.

❸ Riva degli Schiavoni★★

The Serenissima has dedicated one of its most beautiful quays to the Slavs (Schiavoni) of Dalmatia. Forget about the *vaporetti* and ignore the (somewhat rare) traces of modern-day life and you'll feel as if you've stepped into a painting by Canaletto or Guardi.

❹ Santa Maria della Pietà★

Riva degli Schiavoni
☎ 041 523 10 96
May-Oct. Mon.-Fri. 10am-12pm and 4-6pm, Sat.-Sun. 10am-1pm and 4-5.30pm.

Vivaldi, who was the *maestro di cappella* of the Ospedale della Pietà until 1740, wasn't acquainted with the present church, which was rebuilt shortly after his death. Yet the oval room, from which all sharp angles have been banished for acoustic reasons, rings today with the *concerti* of the "red priest" (Vivaldi's nickname). Worth a visit if only to admire the Tiepolo frescoes. If a concert is scheduled, don't hesitate to go!

❺ Church of San Zaccaria★★

☎ 041 522 12 57
Mon.-Sat. 10am-12pm and 4-6pm. Entrance charge for the chapel.
A beautiful Renaissance church, whose internal decorations are just as appealing at its attractive façade. It contains one of the finest, if not *the* finest work by Giovanni Bellini – a Virgin and Child, naturally. In a side chapel (entry charge), 15th-century altarpieces are encrusted with gold, and there are frescoes by the Florentine Castagno.

❼ Scuola di San Giorgio degli Schiavoni★★★

Calle Furlani
☎ 041 522 88 28
Tue.-Sat. and Sun. morning Apr.-Oct. 9.30am-12.30pm and 3.30-6.30pm; Nov.-Mar. 10am-12.30pm and 3-6pm
Entrance charge.
The *scuola* was the official seat of the Confraternità dei Dalmati, a group of tradesmen from the Balkans who did business with the Venetians. Although it contains only ten or so paintings by Carpaccio (including a beautiful representation of St George slaying the dragon), this is one of the major sights of Venice and an absolute must. Nothing has changed here since the 16th century.

❽ Antica Sacrestia restaurant★★

Calle della Sacrestia, 4442
☎ 041 523 07 49
Closed Mon.

Venetians and those who know the town well go there to eat. A small room, richly decorated with paintings, and local dishes (*la cucina dei Dogi* is what the sign by the entrance promises): fried squid, Venetian style cuttlefish served with polenta, salmon marinated in pink peppercorns… and pizzas. No terrace.

❻ CHURCH OF SAN GIORGIO DEI GRECI AND ICON MUSEUM★★

Come to the Orthodox Mass here to breathe in the heady incense and hark back to a time when the Serenissima had a special relationship with Constantinople. In addition, visit the *scuola*, with its rich collection of icons executed by Byzantine artists in Venice after their flight from the Ottoman Empire. You'll be lost in wonder as you stroll through the timeless museum, a large room with a polished wooden floor that creaks satisfyingly underfoot.

Museum: ☎ 041 522 65 81; Every day 9am-4.30pm; Entrance charge
Church: ☎ 041 523 95 69; Mon. and Wed.-Sun. morning 9am-12.30pm, 2-5pm; access from Ponte dei Greci.

12

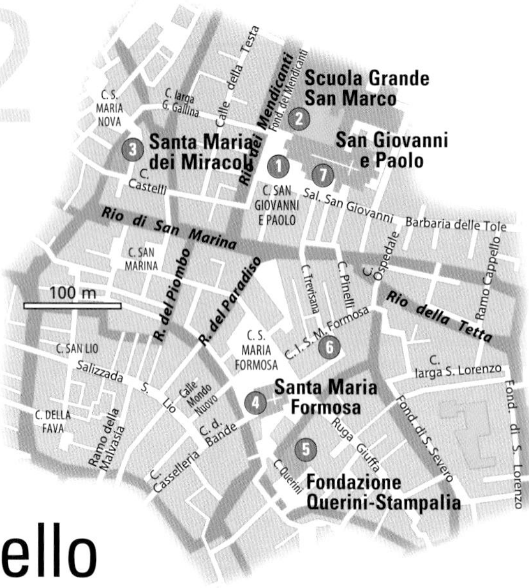

Castello

This district is an astonishing maze. During the day, the *campi* of the Castello welcome fruit or flower stalls and busy shoppers gather in the boutiques. At night, there is a mysterious charm in walking quietly through this district when cats, too, are prowling about.

❶ The statue of condottiere Bartolomeo Colleoni★★★

The great military leader Colleoni bequeathed his immense fortune to the city on the express condition that his equestrian statue be placed in front of San Marco. Reluctant to infringe an old regulation prohibiting building in front of the basilica, the authorities set up Verrocchio's masterly work in front of the Scuola San Marco – and then pocketed the cash!

❷ Scuola Grande San Marco★★

Now the hospital of Venice, the Scuola San Marco has a magnificent asymmetrical façade by Pietro Lombardo decorated with trompe l'œil motifs and marble panels.

❺ Fondazione Querini-Stampalia★★

Campo Santa Maria Formosa 5252
☎ 041 520 34 33
Every day except Mon. 10am-6pm, Fri.-Sat. 10am-10pm
Entrance charge.

This 16th-century *fondazione* stands on a quirky convoluted *campiello* that's a mixture of bridges and canals. The foundation's collection allows you to become better acquainted with the art of Bellini,

Tiepolo and Longhi. But make sure the museum is open, or you'll pay the full entrance fee just to visit the first floor.

❸ Church of Santa Maria dei Miracoli★★

☎ 041 275 04 62
Mon.-Sat. 10am-5pm, Sun. 1-5pm
Entrance charge.

A real gem. The exterior of this recently renovated little Renaissance church is covered with colorful marble panels and the sumptuous interior houses Niccolò di Pietro's Virgin and Child. The whole of the surrounding district is worth a closer look.

❹ Church and Campo of Santa Maria Formosa★★

☎ 041 275 04 62
Mon.-Sat. 10am-5pm and Sun. 1-5pm.
Entrance charge.

This pretty 16th-century church is quite unusual, with its double entrance on a vast *campo* lined with café terraces. The interior, which is very light, houses a *Madonna della Misericordia* (right aisle) by Vivarini that you could never tire of looking at. Close by, the Calle Lunga S. M. Formosa and Calle delle Bande are packed with interesting shops, including a mask-makers.

❻ Al Mascaron★★

Calle lunga S. M. Formosa, 5225
☎ 041 522 59 95
Mon.-Sat. 12-3pm, 7-11pm.

Next to the church of Santa Maria Formosa, this is a *trattoria* with an authentic Venetian atmosphere, decorated with huge wine flasks. The cooking is excellent and the prices are affordable. Try the *pasta e fagioli* (pasta with beans) and the grilled fish.

❼ BASILICA DI SAN GIOVANNI E PAOLO★★★

Always on the lookout for ways of celebrating itself, the Serenissima spared no expense when building and embellishing San Zanipolo (a contraction of the names Giovanni and Paolo). The 13th- to 15th-century church, which was the pantheon of the Doges, is quite breathtaking. No fewer than twenty-five of the powerful men who built Venice lie here side by side. In this sculpture museum, don't miss the tombs of the Doges Mocenigo (right aisle), Vendramin (choir) and Marcelo (left aisle), all of which are by Pietro Lombardo. The interior of the church also houses a staggering quantity of paintings by Bellini, Veronese and Piazzetta.

☎ 041 523 75 10
Mon.-Sat. 9.15am-6.30pm, Sun. 12-6.30pm.
Entrance charge.
See Don't Miss p. 83.

13

Cannaregio

After the crowds on the Rialto Bridge, the wide Strada Nova seems less touristy. The Cannaregio and its long, peaceful *fondamente* unveil another facet of Venice. Don't miss the Ca' d'Oro, a vast collapsed Gothic palace whose marine entrance is constantly bathed by the water of the Grand Canal.

❶ Ghetto Nuovo and Museo d'Arte Ebraica★★

Campo del Ghetto, 2902/B
Museo : Every day except Sat. 10am-5pm (to 7pm Jun. to Sep.)
☎ 041 71 53 59
3 synagogues: guided tours (inquire at the museum); Every day 10.30am-3.30pm (to 5.30pm Jun. to Sep.). Entrance charge.

Entirely surrounded by canals, the Ghetto Nuovo is a vast esplanade surrounded by "skyscrapers" (buildings over five stories high). There are still a few Jewish businesses here (kosher restaurants and craft shops), as well as Ashkenazy synagogues and a museum of Jewish art with gold and silver plate and superb fabrics dating from the 17th and 18th centuries.

❷ Ghetto Vecchio★★

Despite their size, the houses of the Ghetto Vecchio were unable to accommodate the Jewish community after 1540. It therefore spread to the quiet district of the old foundry (*getto*), around the magnificent Spanish synagogue (Scuola Spagnola), with its polished wood interior.

❸ Anice Stellato★

Fondamenta della Sensa, 3272
☎ 041 72 07 44
Wed.-Sun. 12.30am-2.30pm and 7.30-10pm.

This *trattoria* serves delicious Venetian cuisine with an Oriental touch. You should try the black *risotto – al nero di seppia* – prepared with cuttlefish ink: absolutely delicious!

❹ Campo dei Mori★

Here is a tranquil and inspiring *campo* which tells us a lot about Cannaregio. On the *fondamenta* (N°3398) you will see the house of Jacopo Robusti, also known as Tintoretto, who was born in the area. The *campo* itself owes its name to the intriguing Moorish sculptures displayed in the façades of the houses. These Moors were in fact the Mastelli brothers, who originated from Morea in Greece. These silk merchants settled in Venice in 1112. The low-relief sculptures of the Mastelli Palace – opposite Tintoretto's house – are quite remarkable. This district was once occupied by Arabic merchants.

❺ Cantina ai Mori★

Fondamenta ai Mori, 3386
Every day except Sun. 9am-1pm and 4.30-7pm.

Il signore Baffo, a wine merchant by trade, claims that his family has been Venetian for generations. He's descended from an illustrious family, one of whose members, Safiyé, married the Ottoman sultan Murat III. The shop is full of barrels, which house the very best wines of Venetia.

❻ Church of Madonna dell'Orto★★

Campo Madonna dell'Orto
☎ 041 71 99 33
Every day 10am-5pm.

Fans of Tintoretto shouldn't miss this 15th-century church for anything. Behind a red and white façade, the tomb of the painter and a large number of his works are housed.

❼ Strada Nova★

This is the street where the Venetians do their shopping, and where they come to have a Spritz – the town's most popular aperitif – when it's all done. If you want to discover the real Venice, this is the place to come: you won't come across many tourists in the daytime.

❾ Palazzo Labia★

Campo S. Geremia, 275
☎ 041 78 11 11
Visits by appointment Wed.-Fri. 3-4pm.

In the 20th century, this palace gained the reputation of hosting the most outlandish costumed festivals. The fresoes of Tiepolo, undertaken in 1746 and 1747 in the ballroom and hall of mirrors, are worth seeing.

❽ CA' D'ORO★★★

If we could keep only one of the countless palaces strung out along the Grand Canal, it would be this one. The 15th-century Ca' d'Oro, which takes its name from the gold adorning its elegant façade, houses the Franchetti collection. Its loggias offer a stunning view over the Rialto. Apart from the breathtaking room on the first floor, the interior is modern, but if you like paintings and religious bronze statues from the 15th and 16th centuries (see the sublime *Saint Sebastian* by Andrea Mantegna displayed in its original setting), then you will find the Ca' d'Oro one of the most interesting museums in town.

Grand Canal, entrance via calle Ca' d'Oro; ☎ 041 523 87 90
Every day 8.15am-7.15pm, except Mon. 8.15am-2pm;
Entrance charge.

14

The islands of Giudecca and San Giorgio Maggiore

The island of the Giudecca was once called the *spina longa* (the fish bone) because of its elongated shape. It was originally the place to which Venetian families that had been tried and found guilty (*giudicato*) were exiled, and later, in the 16th century, the home of patricians in search of some greenery. It has now become a popular residential district. The embankments offer a nice setting for a quiet walk. On San Giorgio Maggiore the view from the top of the campanile is breathtaking and you won't have to stand in line as you do on Piazza San Marco!

❶ Mulino Stucky★

Closed for restoration.

This enormous, red neo-Gothic flour mill adds a curiously modern, industrial touch to the island of the Giudecca. It bears the name of its former owner, the Swiss Stucky, who was murdered by one of his employees in 1910.

❷ Restaurant Harry's Dolci★★

Fondamenta San Biagio, 773
☎ 041 522 48 44
Apr.-Oct. Wed.-Sun. 12-3pm and 7-11pm.

An offshoot of Harry's Bar (see p. 96), this restaurant is very pleasant when the sun is shining, and the check will turn out to be slightly less ruinous in comparison. This is the place to sample a Bellini or a delicious pastry in the company of Venetian polite society.

❸ Mistra★

Fondamenta San Giacomo, 212/A
☎ 041 522 07 43
Every day except Mon. evening and Tue.

Well off the beaten track and far from the main tourist areas, this restaurant's originality is due to the fact that it is located on the second floor of an old dockyard. You'll get a splendid view from the iron staircase. They serve a variety of international, Ligurian and Venetian dishes.

❹ Church of Rendentore★★

Campo Redentore
☎ 041 275 04 62
Mon.-Sat. 10am-5pm, Sun. and holidays 1-5pm
Entrance charge.

This collection of pure geometrical shapes was built by Palladio following the end of the plague of 1576 that wiped out a third of the population of Venice. Every year on the *festa del Rendentore* (see p. 20), a bridge made out of boats is set up over the Canale della Giudecca from the Zattere opposite.

❺ Convent of Zitelle★

Fondamenta delle Zitelle, 32
☎ 041 271 90 12
Apr.-Oct. Fri.-Sat. 3.30-6.30pm.

Designed by Palladio and crowned with the obligatory dome, the church owes its name to the old maids (*zitelle*) of the convent next door, who were said to be skilled lacemakers. Behind the church, on the south side of the island, is one of Venice's most notable hotels, the Cipriani, with its terrace opening onto the lagoon.

❻ Tre Oci★

Fondamenta delle Zitelle, 43
Closed to the public.

This strange neo-Gothic palace, which was built by a painter in the early 20th century, owes its name to the three curious windows that look out over the Canale della Giudecca.

❼ Giorgio Cini Foundation★★★

☎ 041 520 55 58
Every day 10am-6.30pm
Only open during exhibitions.
Entrance charge.

This foundation occupies the major part of the small island of San Giorgio Maggiore, and particularly the Church's old convent and cloisters (the cloister of the laurels and the cloister of the cypress trees). If by chance they are organizing a concert, an exhibition or a play during your stay, don't hesitate to go. You won't regret it.

❽ CHURCH OF SAN GIORGIO MAGGIORE★★★

This church is a lesson in architecture. Once again, and even more so than before, Palladio will delight you with his admiration for the forms of Ancient Rome. It's difficult not to be moved in the face of such conviction, although the interior, which houses important works by Tintoretto (choir and sacristy), is somewhat overpowering and a little bit cold as well. Make a beeline for the top of the bell tower. There, in the company of a monk, you'll have an absolutely fabulous view of the lagoon, which is even finer than the one from the campanile of Piazza San Marco.

☎ 041 241 47 17; Every day 9.30am-12.30pm and 3-5pm (2-6.30pm in summer)
Entrance charge (elevator) to the bell tower.

15

The island of Murano

With its canal, which is large only in name, its comparably modest palaces and fewer churches, Murano is like a miniature version of Venice. Everything here revolves around the glass manufacturing industry of which it is so proud.

❶ Museo dell'Arte Vetraria or Museo Vetrario★★

Fondamenta Giustinian, 8
☎ 041 73 95 86
Every day except Wed. 10am-5pm (ticket office closes at 4.30pm)
Entrance charge.

The Palazzo Giustinian (17th century) is so interesting that you'll soon forget the less than lively presentation. Besides gaining an insight into the development of Murano glass and the various techniques used in its manufacture, you can see the creations of

the greatest masters of the art, beginning with Angelo Barrovier (1405–1460). After admiring all these treasures, you'll undoubtedly view the island's shopwindows with a new perspective.

❷ Church of Santa Maria e Donato★★★

Campo San Donato, 11
☎ 041 73 90 56
Every day 8am-12pm and 2-6pm (7pm in summer)
Entrance free.

You can't help wondering why this 12th-century church has its back to the canal, but the reason is in fact simple – the apse which reflects in the water. The interior isn't so bad, either. Besides the mosaic on a gold background in the apse, the church has incredible paving.

❸ Palazzo Trevisan★

Closed to the public

This palace, attributed to Palladio, is the finest on the island and definitely the equal of the well-known Palazzo Giustinian opposite.

❹ Church of San Pietro Martire★

Campo dei Vetrai
☎ 041 73 97 04. Every day except Sat. am; 9am-6pm.

Although the exterior of this church is not exactly memorable, it's worth paying a visit to see its many works of art, some of which are lit by chandeliers (Murano glass, of course). These include a Madonna by Bellini, canvases by Veronese and Tintoretto and many other wonders.

❺ Mazzega

Fondamenta da Mula, 147
☎ 041 73 68 88
Ⓕ 041 73 90 79
Every day 9am-5pm.

Opposite the Ponte Vivarini, a showroom of one of the great names of Murano glass displays a stunning collection of its finest creations, past and present. The vases, services, chandeliers and antique jewelry on display make an incredible sight. If you think (quite rightly) that all this could make a considerable dent in your bank account, think of it as an investment and you won't regret it. The workshop is just next door and is open to visitors.

❻ Trattoria Ai Frati★

Fondamenta Venier, 4
☎ 041 73 66 94
Every day except Thu. 12-3pm. Closed for the 3 weeks following the Carnival.

A tourist restaurant serving good traditional Venetian cuisine. Sit on the terrace and order an *anguilla sull'ara* (baked eel) – it's quite delicious.

THE GLASS GALLERIES

The gallery floors are entirely covered in Murano glass mosaics. Various glass works designed by young contemporary artists are exhibited next to mirrors created by Philippe Stark and original-looking glass goblets. There is so much to see here there can be no excuse for not visiting the island's galleries. We particularly recommend you visit Andromeda (Fondamenta Vetrai, 58; ☎ 041 73 68 01; see also pp. 114–115.)

16

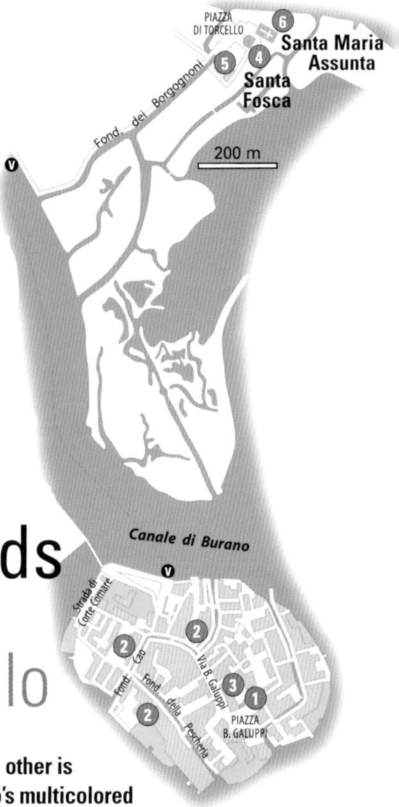

The islands of Burano and Torcello

One island is lively, while the other is delightfully nostalgic. Burano's multicolored houses line the banks of the small canals. Torcello, which was the capital of the lagoon until the 10th century, now has only a handful of inhabitants. Wild and isolated, the island would probably be completely deserted if its ancient cathedral wasn't there to attract visitors.

ISLAND OF BURANO

❶ Scuola dei merletti★★

Piazza Galuppi, 187
☎ 041 73 00 34
Every day except Tue. 10am-5pm. Entrance charge.

You really should visit Burano's lace (*merletti*) museum first before rushing into buying anything. Pay special attention

to the final projects of the school of lacemakers. Each of them took several months to make and can be compared to the work of a goldsmith. If you then go and check out the lace goods on sale in the Via Galuppi they're sure to suffer by comparison.

❷ The fondamente and the houses★★

Fishermen used to paint their houses in bright colors so that they could spot them from a distance. The most attractive groups of these simple dwellings aren't to be found in the most crowded place – along the street dedicated to the local

celebrity, the musician Baldassare Galuppi (1706–1785), known as "Il Buranello" – but rather by the side of simple *fondamente* (such as the Fondamenta della Giudecca) or little *calle*.

❸ Trattoria Da Romano★★

Via San Martino Destro, 221
☎ 041 73 00 30
Every day except Tue. and Sun. evening; 12-3pm and 6-9pm (summer only).

One of the most famous restaurants in the lagoon. Here you'll find an

incomparable choice of fish (eel, dory, monkfish, sole and sardines) – each cooked with skill in a variety of ways – as well as soup, *risotto* and fried dishes. Reservations essential in summer and at the weekend because of tour groups.

ISLAND OF TORCELLO

❹ Church of Santa Fosca★

Every day 10am-12pm and 2-6.30pm.

Squat and round (though octagonal on the outside), this church is entered via a magnificent portico. Its architecture harks back to the dawn of Christianity, yet it's a contemporary of its neighbor.

❺ Locanda Cipriani★★

Piazza Santa Fosca, 29
☎ 041 73 01 50
Every day except Tue. 12am-3pm, Fri.-Sat. 7-9.30pm.

One of the lagoon's major restaurants. The house dishes include pasta stuffed with meat, *risotti*, fish and seafood. There are also six rooms so you can spend a peaceful night on the island.

❻ Church of Santa Maria Assunta★★★

☎ 041 73 00 84
Apr.-Sep. Every day 10.30am-5.30pm; Oct.-Mar. Every day 10.30am-12.30pm and 2-5pm. Entrance charge to church, bell tower and archeological museum.

Ernest Hemingway was delighted by this old cathedral (built in 639) and it's not difficult to see why. Its mosaics (12th and 13th centuries) are

some of the most important examples of Byzantine art; the *Last Judgment* (wall 0), portrays with sadistic pleasure the torments of the damned and would have appealed to Bosch and Bruegel. Note the elegant marble pulpit and the iconostasis, the latter decorated with symbolic animals.

HOW TO GET THERE

Take the NL boat in Fondamente Nove, in the Cannaregio. The crossing to Burano takes about forty minutes. From there, another boat will take you in five minutes to Torcello. When you land, make a note of the return times. The "Laguna tour" ticket (about €8.5) is valid all day long. If you wish, you can combine your visit with that of Murano, either on your way there or on the way back. From Burano, another line will take you to the Lido.

Piazza San Marco

Until the 12th century, Venice's most famous piazza was occupied by the San Zaccaria convent. In 1723, it was transformed into a gigantic paved ballroom. The city's life has always revolved around this square, the difference being that today one is more likely to meet tourists and pigeons.

The Procuratie

In the past, the Procuratie were the official residence of the town's dignitaries. They were so famous that French architect Victor Louis visited them while in search of ideas for the Palais Royal in Paris. Under their splendid arcades, you'll find numerous shops.

The Campanile

This tower, nearly 90m (300ft) tall, offers a fantastic view of the whole city. In the 12th century, it was a lighthouse for the ships of the Adriatic sea. It then became a prison in the Middle Ages. It collapsed in 1902, and ten years were needed to put it back together again.

The clock tower

At the end of the Procuratie Vecchie stands the clock tower with its superb lion, the symbol of Venice. Bronze figurines representing the Mori strike the hours with small mallets. The performance of these mechanical puppets during Ascension week is even more spectacular, when the Angel and the Magi come to pay homage to the Virgin and Child.

The cafés

In order to enjoy the magic atmosphere of the piazza in optimal conditions, sit at a table in one of its famous cafés: the Lavena, the Quadri or the Florian. In the warm season, if you are fortunate, you might even hear a chamber music concert.

INFORMATION

Piazza San Marco (see p. 40).

Basilica di San Marco

Just as impressive from the inside as from the outside, the San Marco Basilica with its characteristic Greek cross shape dates back to the 11th century. It contains innumerable works of art. More than 4,000² m (40,000² ft) of mosaics decorate its five golden domes and floors.

The exterior

Above the Basilica's huge portal is a 17th-century mosaic, representing the theft of the relics of St Mark. The surrounding sculptures represent the labors of the 12 months of the year. On the right side, you can still see the statue of the four Tetrarchs, sculpted in the 4th century, as well as the famous bronze horses which dominate the huge square and seem to be looking over the city.

The Pala d'Oro

Hidden in half-obscurity behind the master altar stands the *Pala d'Oro*, the Basilica's most extraordinary and most precious masterpiece. Two hundred and fifty gold panels, eighty enameled figures and more than three thousand precious stones make up this superb retable, from which Christ, on his throne, the Virgin and the Apostles who stand on his sides, have been looking over the faithful since 1345.

The treasure

Following the looting of Constantinople in 1204, numerous sculptures in silver and gold were brought back to Venice. Among its most precious possessions are the incense burner, the golden chalice and the icon representing St Michael.

INFORMATION

Basilica di San Marco
(see p. 40)
Piazza San Marco
☎ 041 522 52 05
Every day 9.30am-5pm, Sun. 2-4pm
Entrance charge for the *galleria*.

Palazzo Ducale

The Doges' Palace is a prime example of the city's Gothic architecture. After several extensive transformations, it reached its final configuration in the 15th century. Seat of the Venetian government, it was also the personal residence of the Doges. Opulent, sumptuous, decorated with countless paintings from the greatest Renaissance masters, it deserves a half-day visit.

The façades

The palace's Gothic façades are a remarkable architectural feat. They were constructed using a medieval technique which supported large structures with the finest pillars. One still wonders how it can hold together. Inside, a courtyard surrounded by magnificent sculpted façades opens onto the imposing Giants' Staircase which leads to the loggias.

The Hall of the Grand Council

It's in this hall, the largest in the palace, that the members of the assembly met. Its sculpted ceiling, covered in gold leaf, is adorned with numerous paintings by the famous Bassano, Veronese and Palma the Younger. On the hall's farthest wall, its most impressive masterpiece, *Paradise,* executed by Tintoretto and his son between 1588 and 1590.

Bocca della Verità

Near the golden stairway is a mask-like receptacle, the *Bocca della Verità* or Mouth of Truth. Also called the "Lion's Mouth," it served to encourage the citizens of Venice to leave anonymous accusations about their neighbors. In the 17th century, informers were required to leave their address in order to be allowed to give evidence in the trial. If it transpired that the informer had overstepped the mark or had made a critical mistake, the death penalty could be imposed. This "mailbox" was used frequently during the Inquisition.

INFORMATION

Palazzo Ducale
(see p. 41)
Piazza San Marco
☎ 041 271 59 11
Nov. 1-Mar. 31, every day 9am-5pm; Apr. 1-Oct. 31, every day 9am-7pm. Entrance charge (ticket office closes 1h earlier)

Palazzo Grassi

Overlooking the Grand Canal, this splendid palace belonging to the Grassi family first draws one's attention with its soft pastel colors – its white, green and pink façades strike a particularly original note. Nowadays, the palace is an art gallery of international renown.

Exhibitions
Having become a private foundation, the palace now hosts regular exhibitions on a wide range of subjects. From Leonardo da Vinci to Andy Warhol, Etruscan art, the Futurists, Dalí or early 20th-century Italian art, diversity is the hallmark of this gallery's exhibition program.

The palace's history
In 1735, the Grassi family decided to build a palace on the Grand Canal, following the plans of architect Giorgio Massari. In 1984, the Fiat company bought the palace in order to save it from imminent collapse and restore it to its previous splendor. The restoration was entrusted to Gae Aulenti, who had already illustrated himself working on the Quai d'Orsay Museum in Paris, and Antonio Foscari, a descendent of the Doges. Two years later, it was opened to the public.

The interior
The palace's main staircase is a work of art in its own right. This impressive mass of sculpted marble, decorated with 18th-century frescoes, is the first thing one sees on entering the palace. It's also well worth going for a stroll in the glasshouse.

INFORMATION

Palazzo Grassi
(see p. 45)
Campo San Samuele, 3231, San Marco
☎ 041 523 16 80
Only open during exhibitions (information about current exhibitions is available from the tourist office).

Gallerie dell'Accademia

The Accademia gallery is one of the most prestigious museums in the world, and offers a comprehensive view of Venetian painting from the 14th to the 17th centuries. In spite of a slightly haphazard presentation (artists are not exhibited in chronological order, and space being scarce, paintings are often crammed together), each room is worthy of interest. It would be a shame not to pay a visit.

Rooms IV and V

The paintings exhibited in these two rooms might be rather small is size, they are nevertheless highly remarkable. Next to the works of Mantegna and Giorgione, one finds fifteen wood panel paintings of the great Venetian master Giovanni Bellini, such as a beautiful *Virgin and Child*. Giorgione's *Old Woman* and *The Storm* are also extraordinary.

Room XXI

This room is entirely occupied by Carpaccio's series of eight large paintings dedicated to the life of Saint Ursula. He was famous for paying great attention to realistic detail and integrating them in a dream-like atmosphere.

Ponte dell'Accademia

Opposite the gallery, the Accademia Bridge leads to San Marco. Built by the Austrians in 1854, its metallic structure was replaced by a wooden bridge in the nineteen thirties. What was then meant to be a temporary installation became permanent and was entirely restored in 1985. The view over the Grand Canal is splendid.

INFORMATION

Accademia gallery
(see p. 50)
Campo della Carità
☎ 041 522 22 47
Tue.-Sun. 8.15am-7.15pm, Mon. 8.15am-2pm. Entrance charge (ticket office closes 45 minutes earlier)

Rio and Squero San Trovaso

The Rio San Trovaso leads from the Grand Canal to the Zattere, which run along the Giudecca Canal. Walking along this charming *rio* you will discover the Dorsoduro district, a quiet and picturesque area of Venice, which seems to have hardly changed at all since the 18th century.

Squero San Trovaso

This workshop specializes in the construction and the repair of gondolas. Built in the 17th century, it is the oldest surviving workshop in Venice. Nowadays, only ten gondolas are built there every year. The premises are closed to the public, and it's unfortunately quite unlikely that you will see a gondola, but the building itself with its small wooden huts is very interesting, even from the outside.

The Zattere

Located at one end of the Rio San Trovaso, the Zattere (literally: the pontoons, the docks) is an ideal place to eat an ice cream while looking at the Giudecca island on the other side of the canal.

San Trovaso Church

After having been destroyed by fire, this church was entirely rebuilt in 1590, in the neo-classical style. It contains wonderful paintings by Tintoretto and Palma the Younger.

Gondolas

Venice's traditional means of transportation, gondolas are all handmade, following a technique which was perfected until the late 19th century. Their structures are made using nine different types of wood and painted over with seven layers of black lacquer. Their structure is asymmetrical – one of the sides is 12cm (5 inches) longer than the other – to help balance these single-oar embarkations. In the past, Venice's canals were home to more than 14,000 gondolas. Today, there are no more than 400 left.

INFORMATION

Rio and Squero San Trovaso (see p. 51)
Church: every day except Sun.
8-11am and 3-6pm
☎ 041 522 21 33.

Peggy Guggenheim Foundation

Located between the Santa Maria della Salute church and the Accademia gallery, the Peggy Guggenheim Foundation is another highlight of Venice's artistic heritage. Blessed with a magnificent setting, it contains one of the most impressive modern art collections in Europe.

Palazzo Venier dei Leoni

Originally meant to be four stories high, the palace only could afford one floor in the end, as funds for its construction had run out, hence its nickname: the unfinished palace. Peggy Guggenheim, the eccentric American millionaire, found its originality so irresistible that she bought it in 1949. Invisible from the outside, the building's internal courtyard contains a luxuriant garden.

A life's collection

Satisfying her lifelong passion for contemporary art, Peggy Guggenheim collected more than 200 paintings and sculptures between 1938 and 1947. Her life was an uninterrupted series of encounters with extraordinary men and artists. Her second husband was Max Ernst, the surrealist painter. Most of the works of art in the collection were purchased directly from the artists, whom she knew personally.

Cubism, futurism and surrealism

In this temple dedicated to 20th-century painting and sculpture, all the great masters of modern art are represented: Picasso, Magritte, Pollock, Miró, Dalí, Ernst, Mondrian, Kandinsky. The Foundation has a collection worthy of a great European museum. It represents a superb panorama of the last century's creation.

INFORMATION

Peggy Guggenheim Foundation
(see p. 52)
Palazzo Ca' Venier dei Leoni, Dorsoduro 701
☎ 041 240 54 11
www.guggenheim-venice.it
Foundation and museum shop, every day except Tue.10am-6pm.
Entrance charge.

Santa Maria della Salute

Right on the tip of the Dorsoduro district, where the town's two main canals meet, stands Santa Maria della Salute. This extraordinary example of Venetian Baroque is the work of architect Baldassare Longhena, who devoted 50 years of his life to its realization.

The exterior

This building was dedicated to the Virgin Mary as a sign of gratitude for putting an end to the plague which devastated the city in 1630. Its octagonal structure supports a gigantic dome. Every November 21, a procession is organized in honor of the Virgin Mary, during which Venetians cross the Grand Canal on a bridge made of boats.

The interior

The star-shaped pavement of the church leads onto six chapels. At its center, the master altar is decorated with paintings by Tiziano and Tintoretto. To mention but two of the remarkable art works on display: a 12th-century icon of the Madonna della Salute, and Tintoretto's *Feast of Cana* in the sacristy.

The customs office

Located on the right as you come come out of the church, this building was erected in 1677 to house the customs office whose purpose was to check ships' merchandise as they entered the city. Be sure not to miss the weather vane which sits on top of the building: a rotating representation of fortune, standing on a globe supported by two bronze atlantes. The view on San Marco at sunset is very beautiful.

INFORMATION

Santa Maria della Salute church (see p. 53)
Campo della Salute
☎ 041 274 39 11
Every day 9-12am, 3-6pm.

Scuola Grande di San Rocc
Basilica di S. Maria dei Frar

Wandering off into the maze of narrow streets of the San Polo and Santa Croce districts, away from the crowded Rialto, is a delightful experience. One can discover beautiful *campi* and picturesque buildings alongside masterpieces of Venetian architecture such as Scuola Grande di San Rocco and Basilica di Santa Maria dei Frari.

Scuola Grande di San Rocco...

Built in the beginning of the 16th century, this scuola is like a temple dedicated to the work of Tintoretto. The second floor is particularly spectacular. Tintoretto covered all the available surfaces with paintings representing scenes and characters from the Old Testament.

...and its Crucifixion

The atmosphere of the Sala dell'Albergo, the last room on the third floor of the Scuola, is haunting, with its dramatic Crucifixion. Its vigorous brush strokes and contrasted light effects changed the course of Western European painting when Tintoretto completed it in 1565.

Basilica di Santa Maria dei Frari

This red-brick Gothic basilica is home to a great number of art works, the tomb of Tizano and those of several Doges. The heart of Canova is also kept there. It contains Tiziano's *Assumption* and Giovanni Bellini's triptych of the Virgin. Don't miss the friars' choir and its wonderful wood sculptures, the work of Marco Cozzi.

INFORMATION

Scuola Grande di San Rocco (see p. 58)
Campo San Rocco
Scuola: every day Apr.-Oct. 9am-5.30pm, Nov.-Mar. 10am-4pm
☎ 041 523 48 64
Entrance charge (the ticket office closes 30 minutes earlier)
Church: every day 7.30-12.30am; winter: Mon.-Wed. 7.30-12.30am, Sat.-Sun. 7.30-12.30/2-4
☎ 041 523 48 64.
Basilica di Santa Maria dei Frari (see p. 59)
Campo dei Frari
☎ 041 275 04 62
Mon.-Sat. 9am-6pm, Sun. 1-6pm.
Entrance charge.

Ca' Rezzonico

The Ca' Rezzonico is also known as the museum of 18th-century Venetian art. This luxurious palace was acquired in 1712 by a family of rich bankers, the Rezzonicos. They entrusted the completion of this ambitious architectural project to Massari. This museum, with its wonderful collection of works by Longhi, Canaletto, Piazzetta and Guardi, is a perfect introduction to Venice's glorious 18th century.

The library
In the second floor library, you can see an interesting document: a letter granting the Rezzonico family their titles of nobility, in exchange for the payment of 100,000 ducats.

The third floor
This floor contains several 18th-century masterpieces, such as the *Rhinoceros* of Pietro Longhi, *Il Ridotto* and *Il Palatorio* by Guardi. It also has a collection of oriental-style furniture and a sculpted harpsichord.

The ballroom
Designed by Massari and decorated by Visconti and Crosato, this spectacular room covers the whole area of the palace and is two stories high. The first ball was given in 1758 and firmly established the family's reputation and fame. Its collection of Brustolon furniture is quite extraordinary. Concerts are held here.

The room of the Nuptial Allegory
This room contains a beautiful fresco by Tiepolo in 1757, which celebrates the wedding of Ludovico Rezzonico.

INFORMATION

Ca' Rezzonico
(see p. 55)
Fondamenta Rezzonico, 3136
☎ 041 241 01 00
Every day except Mon. 10am-6pm.
Entrance charge.

Ponte di Rialto

Having walked around San Marco Square, visitors usually move onto the Rialto district, and to the famous bridge which for many centuries was the business center of Venice. Numerous souvenir shops draw large crowds in the daytime. In the evenings, the bridge offers a wonderful view of the illuminated Grand Canal.

The bridge

Until 1854, this bridge was the only means of crossing the Grand Canal on foot. It was taken down and rebuilt several times between the 12th century, when it was first built, and the 16th century, when it was given its final configuration. Conceived by Antonio da Ponte, its complex structure called for ingenious construction work. Its arch, which is 7.5m (23ft) high, is supported on both sides by more than 6,000 submerged pillars.

The markets

The market starts at the bridge. If you walk around the market area, you will come across the most famous market stalls in Venice. The Erberia specializes in the sale of fruits and vegetables. In the Pescheria, you will find fresh fish and seafood which come directly from the fishermen's docks on the Grand Canal.

San Giacomo di Rialto

The San Giacomo di Rialto church is only a short walk away from the Rialto Bridge. Of the church itself, only the columns, their capitals and a clock tower remain. The latter is well worth seeing. With its Roman numerals and its golden hands which have been turning around a representation of the sun since 1410, the clock has been a local attraction for centuries.

INFORMATION

Ponte di Rialto
(see p. 56).

San Giovanni e Paolo

Facing the Scuola Grande di San Marco, Venetians refer to the Basilica di San Giovanni e Paolo simply as "San Zanipolo." Its Gothic style is similar to that of the Santa Maria dei Frari church. The Dominicans built the church at the end of the 13th century. It is home to the tombs of 25 Doges, all adorned with remarkable sculptures.

The church

First, the unfinished façade with its portal by Bartolomeo Bon, which leads into a gigantic hall. Inside, various works of art, all remarkable: sculpted tombs, paintings by Bellini, a retable by Lorenzo Lotto, three chapels, a sacristy dedicated to the Dominicans, a large Murano stained-glass window.

The nave

The proportions are impressive – more than 100m (300ft) long and 30m (100ft) wide! The nave is so large that it had to be given additional support with the introduction of sculpted wooden pillars. The size of its nave makes this church one of the largest Christian sanctuaries in the world.

Statue of Colleoni

On the San Giovanni e Paolo campo stands a statue of Bartolomeo Colleoni. This mercenary, a great historical figure of the Venetian Republic, expressed the wish, just before dying, of having his statue erected on the city's largest square. In exchange for this honor, he would bequeath all that he owned to the city he had served. In 1488, ten years after his death, his last wish was fulfilled.

INFORMATION

San Giovanni e Paolo Basilica
(see p. 63)
☎ 041 523 75 10
Every day 9.15am-6.30pm, Sun. 12am-6.30pm. Free entrance.

Practicalities

Rates

There are six categories of hotel in Venice, ranging from one star (often called *pensione*) to five stars. They're all expensive. For basic facilities (en-suite shower and bathroom), expect to pay from €100 to €150. For a more comfortable room (with bath, direct phone, television and pleasant surroundings) and room service, you have to pay at least €130. These prices are for a double room in peak season. Off-season rates apply from December to late January only and can save you up to 50 percent off normal prices.

Reservations from home

You can reserve a room through a tour operator to take advantage of better support and sometimes better prices, though you can reserve direct if you go about it early enough (around 2 months in advance in general and up to 6 months if your stay coincides with the Carnival). Phone or fax the hotel to find out what to do. Of course you can also make a reservation on the Internet. Websites such as www.octopustravel.com allow you to reserve rooms instantly online using a credit card. The advantage in this method is that you can immediately find out the availability of rooms and easily compare hotel facilities and prices.

Arriving with no reservation

Don't wander around the city. Go straight to the tourist information office at the station or airport, where they'll find you somewhere to stay. You can also contact the Associazione Veneziana Albergatori (the Association of Venitian Hotelkeepers): palazzo Fontana, 3829, Cannaregio, ☎ 041 522 80 04 or 800 843 006 from Italy

Choosing a district

The hotels near Piazza San Marco are mainly luxury

WATCH OUT FOR THE CHECK!

In Italy, and particularly in Venice, prices are often indicated per 100 grams rather than per kilo.
At the baker, the cake shop, the grocery store or in the delicatessen, you may sometimes find that prices are abnormally cheap: Watch out! Look carefully and you are sure to notice *etto* written on the label, which means hectogram (100g).

ACQUA ALTA

In the fall and winter, the high tides (*acqua alta*) regularly flood Venice and many palazzos have their first floors submerged under water. Everyone then puts on their galoshes or manages to walk as best as they can on footbridges. The town is covered in a few centimeters of water, sometimes up to 1m (3ft). Or more: Venetians remember the 194cm (76in) in November 1966 (the record), and 147cm (57in) in November 2002. In the hope of preserving the city (the sea level is rising and Venice is inexorably sinking), the Italian government adopted the Moses project in 2001, which plans to build 79 mobile locks at the three entrances to the lagoon, which would be shut when the tide goes above a certain level. The work should last for around eight years.

establishments (3-5 stars). On the other hand, the poetical out-of-the-way districts, especially Dorsoduro and Cannaregio, are full of quiet, often charming, little hotels that are less expensive in general than their equivalents in the city center. As Venice isn't very spread out, they're your best bet if you don't want to stay in a luxury hotel.

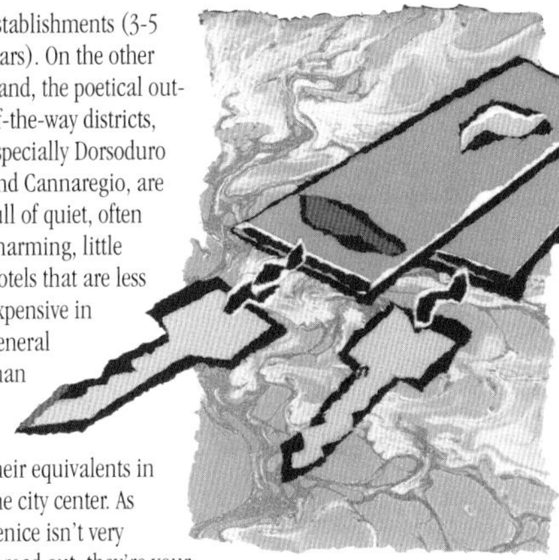

Ristorante, trattoria, bacaro or osteria

You can still have pizzas in a *pizzeria*, but there's now very little difference between a *ristorante* and a *trattoria* (which used to be more informal and less expensive). The *osteria* or *bacaro* is the Venetian equivalent of a wine bar. Some close early in the evening (around 10pm or even earlier). Most places have a few seats, but the Venetians mainly come here for a quick bite of *cicheti* (a variety of little snacks) and an *ombra* (a glass of wine) standing at the bar. The atmosphere is fantastic. You can also have a *tramezzino* (triangular sandwich) and a beer in a *birreria* or a hot meal in a *rosticceria* (steakhouse).

Where to eat

The nearer a restaurant is to Piazza San Marco, the more expensive it's likely to be. It's better to head for the outlying districts (Cannaregio, Santa Croce, Dorsoduro, etc.), where the cuisine is better, price for price. The set meals for tourists are flavorless and should be avoided (especially around the railroad station). Most eating places are shut on Sundays.

Mealtimes

Lunchtime is from noon/1pm to 3pm and dinnertime from 8pm to 9.30pm. It's a good idea to reserve a table in advance, especially at well-known places. Otherwise, arrive before the rush, at around 7/7.30pm.

Meals and prices

A complete meal consists of five courses (see p. 31): the *antipasti* or starter (ham, soup, etc.), the *primo* (pasta) and the *secondo piatto* (meat or fish), the *contorni* (salad or vegetables served separately) and the *dolci* (desserts). Unless you have a huge appetite, three courses are quite sufficient. The cost per person, without wine, is around €20 in an *osteria* and €50 in a smart restaurant. These prices include the *coperto* (cover charge + bread), service (10 percent) and a tip or *mancia* (5 percent or more). In this guide, we indicate prices with the following use of stars:

★ = €10-20
★★ = €20-45
★★★ = more than €45.

FINDING YOUR WAY

Next to each address in the Where to stay, Shopping and Going Out sections, we have given details of the nearest *vaporetti* stop in parenthesis.

Hotels

1 - Europa e Regina
2 - Bonvecchiati
3 - La Residenza

San Marco

Kette★★★★

Piscina S. Moisè, 2053 (Vallaresso)
☎ 041 520 77 66
Ⓕ 041 522 89 64.

A pleasant place to stay on a quiet, not far from La Fenice theater. Cozy, comfortable rooms. Prices more reasonable in winter.

Luna★★★★★

Calle dell'Ascensione, 1243 (Vallaresso)
☎ 041 528 98 40
Ⓕ 041 522 54 09.

A wonderful hotel occupying the former seat of the Templars. It has a lounge with 18th-century frescoes and impeccable rooms with a view of the church of S. Giorgio Maggiore.

Ala★★★

Campo S. M. del Giglio, 2494, S. Marco (Giglio)
☎ 041 520 83 33
Ⓕ 041 520 63 90.

Located halfway between the Piazza San Marco and the Accademia, this quiet hotel has comfortable, sober-styled rooms overlooking a pretty *campo*, a meeting place for gondoliers.

Cavalletto e Doge Orseolo★★★★

Calle Cavalletto, 1107 (Vallaresso)
☎ 041 520 09 55
Ⓕ 041 523 81 84.

A small luxury hotel standing in the delightful Bacino Orseolo, a stone's throw from Piazza S. Marco. You'll be lulled by the serenades of the gondoliers just below. It's the ideal place to spend your honeymoon.

Concordia★★★★

Calle larga di S. Marco, 367 (Vallaresso)
☎ 041 520 68 66
Ⓕ 041 520 67 75.

If you must have a view of the Piazza San Marco (there is a

partial view of the basilica from the breakfast room), then this is the hotel for you. Unfortunately, the rooms are a little lacking in character.

Europa e Regina★★★★

Via larga XXII Marzo, 2159 (Vallaresso)
☎ 041 520 04 77
Ⓕ 041 523 15 33.

A sumptuous palace, which was frequented by Turner and Monet among others, with a fine terrace and a pleasant restaurant on the Grand Canal, where you can dine with a view of the Church of S. Maria della Salute.

Monaco e Grand Canal★★★★

Calle Vallaresso, 1332 (Vallaresso)
☎ 041 520 02 11
Ⓕ 041 520 05 01.

An elegant, luxury hotel with a façade on the Grand Canal overlooking the churches of S. Maria della Salute and S. Giorgio Maggiore. There is mpeccable service and few groups.

Bonvecchiati★★★★

Piazza San Marco, Calle Goldoni, 4488 (Rialto)
☎ 041 528 50 17
Ⓕ 041 528 52 30.

A charming hotel with a great location near Piazza San Marco that's a little expensive for its category. It has sumptuous glass chandeliers and there are modern paintings throughout.

Flora★★★

Calle larga XXII Marzo, 2283/A (Giglio)
☎ 041 520 58 44
Ⓕ 041 522 82 17.

Pleasant and centrally located (minutes from Piazza S. Marco), with a rather old-fashioned decor. The Liberty staircase gives access to small rooms overlooking a quiet courtyard.

La Fenice et des Artistes★★★

Campiello Fenice, 1936 (Giglio)
☎ 041 523 23 33
Ⓕ 041 520 37 21.

A charming *campiello* close to La Fenice theater is home to one of the nicest hotels in the S. Marco district. It's quiet and shady and you can have breakfast in a little courtyard garden. A first-rate hotel.

San Giorgio★★

Rio Terà della Mandola, 3781 (S. Angelo)
☎ 041 523 58 35
Ⓕ 041 522 80 72.

This guesthouse is in San Marco. The 16 romantic small bedrooms – red, green or blue – are tastefully decorated in the Fortuny style (the eponymous palace just next door). Some have a view onto a *rio*. Very warm welcome.

Locanda Fiorita★★

San Marco, 3457 A Campiello Novo (Sant'Angelo or S. Samuele)
☎ 041 523 47 54
Ⓕ 041 522 80 43.

A charming *locanda* just next to the Santo Stefano campo. The quiet, comfortable bedrooms, are furnished in the 17th-century style. Doubles from €110.

San Moisè★★★

Piscina S. Moisè, 2058 (Vallaresso)
☎ 041 520 37 55
Ⓕ 041 521 06 70.

This well-run establishment in the quiet Fenice district offers spacious, personalized rooms furnished in a traditional style. All rooms have en-suite bathrooms, air-conditioning, satellite TV and safes.

Castello

La Residenza★★

Campo Bandiera e Moro, 3608 (S. Zaccaria)
☎ 041 528 53 15
Ⓕ 041 523 88 59.

A superb 15th-century palace with its original decor intact (frescoes in the lounges), in a *campo* far from the crowds. A hotel offering some of the best value for money in Venice.

Locanda La Corte★★★

Castello, 6317
Calle Bressana
(Rialto or Ospedale)
☎ 041 241 13 00
F 041 241 59 82.

Right next to the SS Giovanni e Paulo *campi* and Santa Maria Formosa, in a 16th-century renovated palace, 14 bedrooms and 2 suites. The inner courtyard is, like this *locanda*, simple and pleasant. Doubles from €120 in off-season.

Albergo Doni★

Calle del Vin, 4656
(S. Zaccaria)
☎ / F 041 522 42 67.

To the east of Piazza San Marco, riva Schiavoni, in the quiet area of the rio del Vin, a family hotel dating back to the 16th century, where you will find a warm welcome. The 13 bedrooms (four of them en suite) are large and comfortable. Out of season, some of them cost €80. Non-smoking hotel.

Dorsoduro

Locanda San Barnaba★★★

Calle del Traghetto, 2785-86
(Ca' Rezzonico)
☎ 041 241 12 33
F 041 241 38 12.

The owner, a Venetian of Hungarian origin, restored this ancestral palace to turn it into a hotel. The 13 rooms are all different. Some still display their original fresco paintings, while others offer a view on the lovely garden.

Accademia-Villa Maravegie★★★

Fondamenta Bollani, 1058
(Accademia)
☎ 041 521 01 88
F 041 523 91 52.

This 17th-century residence with a flower-filled courtyard on one side and a garden on the other, is one of the most delightful hotels in Venice. Reserve several months in advance and avoid the annex, which is very noisy

Ca' Pisani hotel★★★★

Dorsoduro, 979 A
Rio Terà A. Foscarini
(Accademia or Zattere)
☎ 041 240 14 11
F 041 277 10 61.

A designer-style hotel between the Zattere and the Accademia. Furniture, architecture, lobby: Every little detail is perfect. The design is meant to be contemporary and remind us of the 1930's and 1940's. Solarium and Turkish baths.

La Calcina★★★

Zattere, 780, Dorsoduro
(Zattere)
☎ 041 520 64 66
F 041 522 70 45
la.calcina@libero.it

John Ruskin stayed in this hotel, facing the Giudecca, while he was writing *The Stones of Venice*. A charming setting, ideally located next to the Accademia and the Guggenheim Foundation. When the weather permits, guests can dine on the floating terrace.

Seguso★★

Zattere, 779
(Zattere – B4)
☎ 041 528 68 58
F 041 522 23 40.

A small guesthouse with a view of the Rio S. Vio and Canale della Giudecca, plus fine furniture, embroidered tablecloths, stucco ceilings, Venetian chandeliers, and a garden. The rooms, with or without bathroom, are delightful. A gem.

1 - *Cipriani*
2 - *Locanda San Barnaba*
3 - *La Calcina*
4 - *Seguso*

Santa Croce and San Polo

Marconi ★★★

Fondamenta del Vin, 729, S. Polo (S. Silvestro)
☎ 041 522 20 68
🅕 041 522 97 00.

A splendid residence, which has guest rooms overlooking the Grand Canal. If you like wood paneling and Rococo decoration, then this congenial hotel is for you.

San Cassiano★★★

Calle della Rosa, 2232, S. Croce (S. Stae)
☎ 041 524 17 68
🅕 041 72 10 33.

A 14th-century palace in a district rich in authentic restaurants. Its Oriental carpets, coffered ceilings and lounges with a view of the Ca' d'Oro make it the finest Venetian palace.

Cannaregio

Eden★★★

Rio Terrà della Maddalena, 2357 (S. Marcuola)
☎ 041 524 40 03
🅕 041 72 02 28.

A small, authentic Venetian hotel overlooking a courtyard with its very own old well. On top of this, it's reasonably priced and in a district full of tempting *osterie* (inns). What more could you ask for?

Malibran★★★

Salizzada S. Giovanni Crisostomo, 5864 (Rialto)
☎ 041 522 80 28
🅕 041 523 92 43.

An old house near the Ponte di Rialto, in the quiet square that's home to the Malibran theater. Cozy rooms with 18th-century furniture and pink damask walls.

Island of Giudecca

Cipriani★★★★

Giudecca, 10 (Zitelle – C4)
☎ 041 520 77 44
🅕 041 520 39 30.

One of Venice's largest hotels (and also the most expensive), with luxurious rooms, a sea water swimming pool to cool off in and a high-class restaurant. A must (if you can afford it!).

Restaurants and *osterie*

1 - Antico Martini
2 - Al Bacareto
3 - Alla Riveta
4 - Antico Dolo

San Marco

Antico Martini★★★

Campo S. Fantin, 1983 (Giglio); ☎ 041 522 41 21
Closed Mon. and Wed. lunchtime, and lunchtime in winter.

Ultrasophisticated cuisine to savor by candlelight on a terrace at the foot of La Fenice. Try the sole Martini or the fillet of duck breast with truffles and enjoy one of the 300 wines from the cellar.

Alla Colomba★★★

Piscina di Frezzeria, 1665 (Vallaresso)
☎ 041 522 11 75
Closed Wed. and Thu. lunchtime.

Another unusual restaurant, which resembles a museum (Chagall, De Chirico, Carrà and Poliakoff all paid for their meals here with paintings). You should try the pasta and white bean soup (*pasta con fagioli*).

La Caravella★★★

Via XXII Marzo, 2399 (Vallaresso)
☎ 041 520 89 01
Open every day.

High-class cuisine in a tasteful and distinguished setting. La Caravella has reinvented the art of preparing fish; make sure you try the lobster soup which is quite delicious.

Trattoria do Forni★★★

Calle Specchieri, 457-468 (Vallaresso et Rialto)
☎ 041 523 21 48
Open every day.

A tourist restaurant but excellent

nonetheless. In summer you can savor the house specialty of *rombo* (turbot) with olives, outside in the cool of the evening.

Alla Riveta★

Ponte S. Provolo, 4625
(S. Zaccaria)
☎ 041 528 73 02
Closed Mon.

This small typical restaurant is the perfect place to get an idea of local Venetian cooking, particularly of their fish dishes. *Polpette* (fish balls), sardines and many other specialties: to help you make your choice, everything is displayed on the counter. This is a favorite spot of gondoliers!

A la Campana★

Calle dei Fabbri, 4720
(Vallaresso or Rialto)
☎ 041 528 51 70
Closed Sun.

An authentic and inexpensive little *osteria* where you can sample real Venetian dishes with the locals. You'll get a very warm welcome.

Dorsoduro

Antica Locanda Montin★★

Fondamenta delle Eremite, 1147 (Accademia; 52 and 82, Zattere)
☎ 041 522 71 51
Closed Tue. and Wed. evening.

This good *trattoria* decorated with modern paintings was once the haunt of students and intellectuals, but they've now made way for tour groups. The service isn't always up to scratch, but the garden is very pleasant in summer.

Al Bacareto★★

Salizzada S. Samuele and calle delle Botteghe, 3447 (S. Samuele)
☎ 041 528 93 36
Closed Sat. evening and Sun.

A typical trattoria that's always full to bursting and only a stone's throw from Palazzo Grassi. Simple traditional dishes.

Pizzeria Al Profeta★

Dorsoduro, 2669
Calle Lunga San Barnaba
(Ca' Rezzonico)
☎ 041 523 74 66
Open every day 12-3pm and 7-10.30pm.

This pizzeria has an impressive list of huge, good and cheap pizzas. The bread is homemade, the wine decent, and the terrace-patio wide and quiet. You can be waited on late at night, without any fuss, every day.

San Polo

Antiche Carampane★★★

Rio Terrà delle Carampane, 1911
(S. Silvestro)
☎ 041 524 01 65
Closed Sun. and Mon., and throughout August.

This charming fish restaurant is elegant and refined and the cuisine is simply delicious. You could try prawns accompanied by a smooth polenta, followed by sea bass cooked in parcels and a bottle of the house white wine. Enjoy your meal!

Osteria Antico Dolo★

Ruga Ravano, 778
(S. Silvestro)
☎ 041 522 65 46.

You can sample typical Venetian cuisine here composed entirely of fresh fish. It's the ideal place for a light meal. There's a good choice of local wines and you can expect a very friendly welcome.

Do Spade★

Calle do Spade, 860
(Rialto)
☎ 041 521 05 74
Closed Wed.

Another *osteria* that's retained its charm despite the proximity of the tourist-ridden Ponte di Rialto. With bottles of wine all around, you can either choose from a tempting array of sandwiches, or else opt for a simple, well-prepared meal in the restaurant.

Da Ignazio★

Calle Saoneri, 2749
(S. Tomà)
☎ 041 523 48 52
Closed Sat. and end-July.

A *trattoria* where you can have a leisurely dinner under a vine. The cuisine is good and the tiramisù melts in your mouth.

Vivaldi★

Calle della Madoneta, 1457
(S. Silvestro)
☎ 041 523 81 85
Open every day 11.30am-2.30pm, 7-10.30pm.

You'll find good regional wines, skilfully cooked Venetian specialties and excellent fish dishes in this *osteria* dedicated to the "red priest" (Vivaldi). Moderate prices in a select setting.

Alla Patatina★

Calle Saoneri, 2741
(S. Tomà)
☎ 041 523 72 38
Every day except Sun. 9.30am-3pm, 5-9pm.

An ideal place to eat *polpette* (fish- and meatballs), sample the local vegetable preparations and taste all sorts of specialties. What a shame they close at 9pm!

San Croce

Nono Risorto★★

Sottoportego della Signora Bettina, 2338
(S. Stae)
☎ 041 524 11 69
Closed Wed. and Thu. lunchtime.

Always packed, this restaurant is particularly pleasant in summer, when you can dine under a wisteria beside the *rio*. The pizzas

are said to be the best in Venice. Don't miss the *speck-zucca* (raw ham with pumpkin) in season. The service tends to vary according to the owner's mood at the time.

Alla Zucca★

Ponte del Megio, 1762
(S. Stae)
☎ 041 524 15 70
Closed Sun.

A delightful little restaurant that serves tasty pasta and vegetarian dishes. There's a terrace that's ideal in the summer, where you can have lunch or dinner under a parasol, far from the noise of the city.

Castello

Corte Sconta★★★

Calle del Pestrin, 3886
(Arsenale)
☎ 041 522 70 24
Every day except Sun. and Mon. 12.30-2pm and 7.30-10pm.; Closed end-Jul. to early Aug. and Jan.

A chic, trendy *trattoria* off the beaten tourist track. Gleaming wooden furniture, a magnificent copper bar and, above all, excellent fish dishes (especially *gnocchetti* with swordfish and stuffed squid). In fine weather the tables are set up outside in the courtyard. The favorite restaurant of Hugo Pratt, the creator of Corto Maltese.

Da Franz★★★

Fondamenta S. Isepo, 754
(Arsenale)
☎ 041 522 08 61
Every day 12.30-2pm and 7.30-10.30pm; closed mid-Nov. to Christmas, mid-Jan. to Carnival.

A gourmet restaurant which specializes in fish. They also possess an excellent wine cellar. Be prepared to pay steep prices.

Canaregio

Ai Promessi Sposi★

Calle dell'Oca, 4367
(Ca' d'Oro)
☎ 041 522 86 09
Closed Wed.

This *osteria*, with its irresistible charm, is hidden away in a tiny street, ignored by tourists. You should go there to taste the delicious cooking (fish pasta) or to simply have a snack at the counter.

4

1 - Da Franz
2 - Alla Zucca
3 - Ca d'Oro
4 - Al Graspo de Ua

Al Graspo de Ua★★★

Calle dei Bombasseri, 5094/A (Rialto)
☎ 041 520 01 50 or 041 522 36 47
Closed Mon. and Sat. lunchtime in summer.

One of the best fish restaurants in the lagoon has opened in this former sacristy. The owner goes shopping every morning and has the reputation of being very fussy about freshness. The soup is excellent.

Ca' d'Oro★★

Ramo Ca' d'Oro, 3912 (Ca' d'Oro)
☎ 041 528 53 24
Closed Thu., Sun. lunchtime and throughout Aug.

Alla Vedova (the widow) as the Venetians have nicknamed it, is a busy *osteria*, always full of people. In the original 19th-century decor, try the cod *baccalà*, one of the best in Venice.

Bentigodi– Da Andrea★

Calle Sele, 1423-1424 (S. Marcuola); ☎ 041 71 62 69
Closed Sun. evening and Mon.

This small *osteria* located in the heart of the Ghetto has a lot of charm, with its wooden tables and its typically Venetian atmosphere. You can choose your meal at the counter: don't overlook their delicious pea soup, their gnocchi and their house white wine (served in a flask).

Murano

Trattoria Valmarena★★★

Fondamenta Navagero, 31 (Museo-Murano)
☎ 041 73 93 13
Open lunchtime every day.

The best restaurant on Murano has a pleasant garden in summer in which to sample *rombo* (turbot), the house specialty.

Busa alla Tore★★

Campo S. Stefano, 3 (Museo-Murano)
☎ 041 73 96 62
Closed evenings.

A fish restaurant in a medieval palace next to the church of San Pietro. Many tourists come here in season, but it offers good value for money.

Burano

Al Gatto Nero★★

Fondamenta Giudecca, 88 (Burano); ☎ 041 73 01 20
Closed Mon. and Nov.

The setting is pleasant (the restaurant is decorated with paintings), the service is good, if a little distant, and the fish dishes are all excellent.

Bacari and wine bars

1 - *Antico Dolo*
2 - *Mascareta*
3 - *Vino Vino*

San Marco

Al Volto★

Calle Cavalli, 4081
(Rialto)
☎ 041 522 89 45
Every day except Sun.
10am-2.30pm and 5-10pm.

A friendly and busy wine bar, with bottles stacked from the floor to the ceiling. Along with a wide choice of fine wines to accompany the *cicheti*, they also serve many different types of beer. No tables: you'll have to make your way to the bar – through a thick crowd of students, gondoliers and taxi-boat drivers.

Vino Vino★★

Calle della Veste, 2007/A
(Giglio)
☎ 041 241 76 88
Every day except Tue.
10.30am-11.30pm.

A quiet and elegant wine bar, where the musicians of La Fenice congregate. Prices are a little bit high, but the place is so pleasant it's well worth it.

Vini da Arturo★★

Calle degli Assassini, 3656
(S. Angelo)
☎ 041 528 69 74
Every day except Sun.
12-2.30pm and 7-10pm.

A restaurant favored by the Venetian bourgeoisie, who are willing to pay a high price for a salad and one of the best tournedos steaks in Venice!

San Polo

Antico Dolo★

Salizzada San Polo, 778
(S. Tomà); ☎ 041 522 65 46
Every day 12-3pm, 5.30-11.30pm.

This old *bacaro* used to be the meeting place of the Venetian dockers who came to drink a glass of red wine (called an *ombra*: literally, a shadow!) and eat a *cicheto*. Times have changed, prices have gone up, but they still serve delicious fish dishes (try the spaghetti in cuttlefish ink).

Vini da pinto★

Campo Beccarie, 367
(S. Silvestro)
☎ 041 522 45 99
Every day except Mon. 10am-10pm.

In the sunny season, one can have lunch outside in front of the *pescheria* (the Rialto fish market). If you're in the area, just stop for a drink and a snack.

Dorsoduro

Da Codroma★

Dorsoduro 2540
(Ca' Rezzonico)
☎ 041 524 67 89
Every day except Sun. 8am-midnight.

This *bacaro* has kept its original decoration ever since it opened 130 year ago: large chestnut tables, wooden chairs and an antique counter. Generous portions of *cicheti* and sandwiches accompany a very good selection of Venetian and Italian wines. Its warm and friendly atmosphere is highly enjoyable. Live music on Tuesdays (jazz, blues, latin and soul).

Già Schiavi★

Dorsoduro, 992
Fondamenta Nani
(Accademia or Zattere)
☎ 041 523 00 34
Every day until 8pm.

It's not always easy to get over to the bar and the tapas! That is often what is so delightful about the *bacari* at peak hours and at Già Schiavi's this is also a measure of its success. The patrons of this *enoteca* (wine bar) overflow onto the narrow fondamenta Nani in the evening, in a joyful hubbub. Wine only is on sale.

Ai Artisti★

Dorsoduro, 1169/A
Fondamenta del Squero
(Ca' Rezzonico)
☎ 041 523 89 44
Every day until 9pm; closed Sun.

In Venice *bacari* are often a cross between an *osteria* and a bar. In the pleasant Troveso district, this one is both an *osteria* and a wine bar. It offers good salads, a dish of the day, panini or *bruscette*, desserts (excellent) and a selection of red and white wines. Small terrace along the *rio*. Quite a trendy place.

Castello

Mascareta★

Calle lunga S. M. Formosa, 5183
(S. Zaccaria)
☎ 041 523 07 44
Every day 7pm-2am except Wed. and Thu.

Near San Marco, the atmosphere in this *enoteca* is smart. Here you will find an excellent choice of wines as well as temporary exhibitions by local artists.

Al Portego★

Castello, 6015
Calle Malvasia
(Rialto)
☎ 041 522 90 38
Every day 10.30am-10.30pm; closed Sun.

A local *bacaro* where people come for a drink, some tapas (*cicheti* in Venice) made with fresh market produce, toast or a hot dish at lunchtime. You can eat at the bar or in the dining room. It's a stone's throw away from Campo San Luca.

Cafés and ice-cream parlors

1 - *Alle Botteghe*
2 - *Harry's Bar*
3 - *Il Gelatone*

San Marco

Harry's Bar

Calle Vallaresso, 1323 (Vallaresso)
☎ 041 523 57 77
Open every day 12-11pm.

If you were alarmed by the restaurant prices, you can console yourself with a cocktail at Harry's Bar. There are two absolute musts – the Rossini (strawberry juice and champagne, only in season) and the Bellini (peach juice and champagne). Drink them with *pierini* – tiny delicious toasted cheese and ham sandwiches.

Alle Botteghe

Calle delle Botteghe, 3455 (S. Angelo)
☎ 041 522 81 81
Open every day.

A real Venetian bar that's a pleasant place to come for a beer or a spritz (Venetian aperitif) of your choice, accompanied by a variety of sandwiches.

Dal Col

Calle dei Fabbri, 1035 (Rialto)
☎ 041 520 55 29
Open every day.

A café-pâtisserie where you can take a break from shopping and enjoy a slice of apple pie or a croissant with a creamy cappuccino.

Caffè Lavena

Piazza S. Marco, 133 (Vallaresso)
☎ 041 522 40 70
Closed Tue. in winter.

A plush tearoom founded in 1750 to rival its neighbors, the Florian and the Quadri.

With its mirrors, 18th-century atmosphere and memories of Richard Wagner, who was a frequent visitor, the Lavena is one of the great cafés of the square.

Dorsoduro

Da Gino

Piscina Forner, 855/A
(Accademia)
Closed Sun.

This is very much a locals' bar. Along with the television and *grappa*, there are a few seats, which is pretty rare in Venice.

Il Caffè

Campo S. Margherita, 2963
(Ca' Rezzonico)
☎ 041 528 79 98
Closed Sun.

A delightful little café with a 1900's decor. The antique coffee percolator inside still works.

Causin Renato

Campo S. Margherita, 2996
(Ca' Rezzonico)
☎ 041 523 60 91
Closes at 8pm; closed Sun.

An old-fashioned shop that's home to one of the best traditional ice-cream makers in Venice. The house specialty is the aptly named "sublime." In summer, the tables are set up in Campo S. Margherita.

Il Doge

Campo S. Margherita, 3058/A

(Ca' Rezzonico)
☎ 041 523 46 07
Open every day until 1am; Closed Dec.-Jan.

An interesting choice of over 40 flavors and reasonable prices, too, in one of the most delightful *campi* in Venice.

Castello

Birreria Forst

Calle delle Rasse, 4540
(S. Zaccaria)
☎ 041 523 05 57
Closed Sat. and throughout Aug.

A small café in the pleasant Castello district where you can stop for a bite to eat between museum visits. There's a choice of *tramezzini piccanti* (triangular spicy sandwiches on wholemeal bread), a plate of *porchetta* (roasted suckling pig) and lots more besides.

Cannaregio

Al Giubagiò

Fondamente Nuove, 5039
(Fondamente Nuove)
☎ 041 523 60 84
Open every day except Tue.

If you're waiting for a *vaporetto* to take you to the islands (Murano, Burano and Torcello), here's a place well off the beaten tourist track where you can go for a drink in an atmosphere that's entirely Venetian.

Lido

Il Gelatone

Viale Santa Maria Elisabetta, 63/A (Lido)
☎ 041 526 56 46
Open every day; closed Jan.-Feb.

The best ice-cream parlor on the Lido. The *mangia e bevi* (eat and drink) ice cream with fruit and cream is quite delicious after a swim in summer or between movies at the Mostra.

Afternoon tea

1

2

3

4

1 - *Premiata Pasticceria Tonolo*
2 - *Premiata Pasticceria Tonolo*
3 - *Marchini*
4 - *Marchini*

San Marco

Marchini

San Marco, 676
Calle Spadaria
☎ 041 522 91 09
(San Zaccaria)
Open every day except Tue. 9am-8pm.

This place serves the best cakes in Venice according to those in the know, and there is a staggering range to choose from. You will need to order the *morellina*, an unforgettable chocolate cake, two days in advance, but worth it if you have time. Try the *barchette*, strawberry tartlets with cream – they're quite delicious.

Dorsoduro

Toletta di Gozzi Lanza

Dorsoduro, 1192
Calle Toletta
(Accademia)
☎ 041 522 74 51
Open every day.

Cakes, long strands of licorice, tiny confectionery such as the little orange and Cointreau chocolate sticks, and *marrons glacés* can all be eaten on the premises at the counter, surrounded by the sweet scent of vanilla. Alternatively, you can go and savor them along the Zattere, on one of the red benches facing the Grand Canal of the Giudecca. Fondants, shortbread cookies and fruit-shaped marzipan are available to take back home.

Premiata Pasticceria Tonolo

Dorsoduro, 3764 (S. Tomà)
☎ 041 523 72 09
Tue.-Sun. 7am-7pm.

Since 1886, this has been the traditional pâtisserie of Dorsoduro. A delicious smell of chocolate and vanilla wafts from the bakery next door. In the morning, you can have a frothy cappuccino at the counter. And, if your visit coincides with the Carnival, then come and try the *fritole*.

San Croce

Gilda Vio

S. Croce, 784, rio Marin (Riva di Biasio)
☎ 041 71 85 23
Every day except Wed. 7am-8.30pm.

One of the best pâtisseries in Venice can be found in an isolated district on the banks of the Rio Marin. The bakery is opposite the shop and you can watch some of Gilda Vio's delicious concoctions being made, including *crostata di marroni* (a chestnut confectionery) and the unforgettable tiramisù.

Cannaregio

Bruscagrin Il Fornaio

Strada Nova, 3845 (Ca' d'Oro); ☎ 041 522 29 68
Mon.- Sat. 7am-8pm.

This bakery makes an incredible variety of bread and heavenly cakes. Besides the traditional *fritole con crema* (cream doughnuts) and *pan del Doge* (fruit bread with almonds), try the *moretto*, a delicious almond and chocolate confectionery.

PANETTERIE AND *PASTICCERIE*

Bread on one side, cakes on the other: Venetians have always kept them separate, and this is for a very good reason. In the past, bread used to be made in monasteries and by craftsmen whose organization went under the name of *arte*. Breadmaking had specific rules, both for Christians, Sephardis and Orthodox Jews, with the best grains coming from Byzantium as well as from Greece or from the East, in special galleys which were closely monitored. Today, you can rely on the label *produzione propria* which indicates that the goods are baked in house.

Pitteri

Strada Nova, 3843/A (Ca' d'Oro)
☎ 041 522 26 87
Every day 7am-8pm.

The famous *zaletti veneziani* or *con pistacchi* (pistachio-flavored rolls) are so delicious here you don't need to be hungry to eat them, and you can have a cappuccino at the same time. The *baute*, the brightly colored chocolates you find all over Venice before the Carnival, are very good value for money, too.

San Polo

Rizzardini

San Polo, 1415 Campiello dei Meloni (San Silvestroh)
☎ 041 522 38 35
Open every day.

In this elegant bar-cum-*pasticceria*, you'll find traditional Venetian confectionery to enjoy with a cappuccino or even with a *prosecco* (sparkling wine goes very well with sweet things). The famous *ciambella veneziana* (Venetian crown) with its sablé pastry and chocolate curls, or the *cestoni di mandorle* (almonds and marzipan!) will seem finer than anywhere else. You can also find a few sandwiches.

Lido

Sabrina

Via Colombo, 20
☎ 041 526 11 51
Every day 7am-8pm; closed Mon. except in summer.

If you happen to visit the Lido, here is a wonderful address for pastries and confectionery.

Burano

Costantini

S.M. SX, 282 (Burano)
☎ 041 73 55 95
Every day 7am-1pm, 4-7.30pm; closed Wed. and Apr.–May in winter.

This unassuming bakery is tucked away close to Piazza B. Galuppi. Here you'll find the great cake specialty of the island, *esse buranello*, an S-shaped cookie that goes very well with tea.

Practicalities

***Tutto è possibile a Venezia* – everything's possible in Venice – as everyone in the stores will be quick to tell you. You can buy a piece of lacquered furniture, order a personalized Carnival mask or a copy of your favorite painting by Canaletto, fall for a Murano glass chandelier and have it shipped home, or whatever else takes your fancy – business sense comes naturally in a city that has built its wealth on trade.**

Store hours

As a rule, the stores in Venice open every day except Sunday (and sometimes Monday morning) from 9/9.30am to 1pm and from 3/3.30pm to 7 or even 8pm. But these times are only intended as a rough guide – this is Italy and opening times vary according to the season, the kind of store and even the mood of the storekeeper (especially in the case of craftsmen, who may leave a sign saying *chiuso* when they feel like getting some fresh air). Over the Christmas period, at Carnival time and in summer, the mask and Murano glass shops, and tourist shops in general, open on Sundays and don't always close for the sacrosanct midday break anymore.
In other words, if you really want to buy something in a particular store, the best thing to do is to telephone in advance and inquire about hours (those shown in the following pages can vary). Another possibility is to come on Saturday, when shopping is in full swing, between 4 and 8pm.

FINDING YOUR WAY

Next to each address in the Where to stay, Shopping and Going Out sections, we have given details of the nearest *vaporetti* stop in parenthesis.

Where to go

The shopping areas are mainly located in the San Marco district. All around the Piazza, of course, and also in the Mercerie. These long and narrow streets just behind the square are like real shopping

OPEN ALL YEAR ROUND

In the San Marco district, the clothes, jewelry, glass and souvenir shops of every kind open virtually all year round.

arcades. Last but not least, the calle larga XXII Marzo which starts from San Marco to the west and looks like a smaller version of the Parisian Champs-Elysées.

Annual closures

These usually take place in August but can also occur in January, shortly before the Carnival.

Sales

These take place in January and July, from the second week in the month onward, as laid down by Italian law. Look out for the signs saying *sconti* or *saldi*.

Prices

Bear in mind that Venice is the most expensive city in Italy and that they are used to rich tourists spending freely in their stores. However, nobody will try to pull the wool over your eyes and prices are displayed everywhere, except where it would be considered to be bad taste (in luxury jewelry stores, for example). Bargaining isn't really a possibility, except at the Campo S. Maurizio antiques market (see p. 45).

Bulky objects

If you've set your heart on Venetian velvet curtains, a custom-made Fortuny fabric dress, 12 bottles of Prosecco, a Murano glass chandelier or a varnished wooden speedboat and can afford it, nothing could be simpler. The Venetian storekeepers will see to everything – they'll arrange dispatch and take care of any insurance formalities.
The following is a reliable transportation company:

Sattis:
S. Croce, 556
☎ 041 529 91 11.

Customs

For citizens of the European Union, there are no customs formalities to complete. You simply have to produce an invoice showing that duty was paid on the goods in Italy. As a rule, you need the authorization of the Belli Arti, the Italian equivalent of the National Heritage, to export objects over fifty years old and you may be asked to show the permit and invoice when you go through customs.

Counterfeits

Beware of buying fake goods (luggage, etc.) that you're offered. Besides being poor imitations, they may land you with a hefty fine. If your goods are seized, the fine may amount to two and a half times the price of the original item. The penalties are proportional: Customs make a distinction between the professional smuggler and the tourist. But in both cases the goods will be seized.

Men's and women's fashion

In Venice, people go for quality and shopwindows are dazzling. Even if the Doges' city does not compare with Milan – the Mecca of fashion – the best Italian fashion designers can be found in the San Marco district. If you want to buy without waiting for the sales, other more traditional but more reasonably priced boutiques are also beginning to open. Or you can treat yourself unashamedly to some accessories.

La Coupole

Calle larga XXII Marzo, 2366 and 2414 (Vallaresso)
☎ 041 522 42 43
Mon.-Sat. 9.30am-7pm, Sun. 10am-6.30pm.

The Venetian leather and suede specialist stocks famous names for both men and women including Alaïa, Montana, Antonio Fusco, Dolce e Gabbana and V2 by Versace. Also offers a choice of products for children.

Araba Fenice

S. Marco, 1822 (Vallaresso-3)
☎ 041 522 06 64
Every day except Sun. 9.30am-1pm, 3.30-7.30pm.

Everything in this sober, elegant shop – the clothes, the jewelry and the decor –

was designed by a group of artists who placed the emphasis on materials and forms. Every design is exclusive and the items are virtually unique, with only one made of each size. It's also one of the few places in Italy where the majestic jewelry of the Danish designer, Moonies, can be found.

Coin

Salizzada S. Giovanni Crisostomo, 5787, Cannaregio (Rialto)
☎ 041 520 35 81
Every day 9.30am-7.30pm (11am Sun.); closed Sun. in August.

The department store of Venice, where you can browse in peace and get a good overview of Italian fashion. Two of the floors are devoted to ladies' fashion, one to men's and one to the home.

Jade Martine

Campo San Marco, 1645 (Vallaresso-3)
☎ / F 041 521 28 92
Mon.-Sat. 10am-7.30pm, Sun. 11.30am-7pm.

Located just behind San Marco Square, this boutique specializes in fine lingerie, with products carrying the best Italian labels such as La Perla, labels from the international fashion houses like Dior, and also from less well-known brands, whose products are, however, worthy of interest. The staff here is very friendly.

Laboratorio Arte & Costume di Monica Daniele

Calle Scaleter, 2235 (S. Stae or S. Tomà)
☎ 041 524 62 42
Every day 9am-6pm, 9.30pm-midnight Sun. evening.

Old-fashioned dresses, hats, grandmother-style scarves to show off at a party or an evening do. If you look, you will find what you've been dreaming of in Monica Daniele's friendly shop, even old dolls. From €10 (plush toys) to €260 (dresses and suits).

Zazù

San Polo, 2750 Calle dei Saoneri (San Tomà); ☎ 041 71 54 26
Every day 10am-1pm and 3pm-7.30pm.

Halfway between affordable ready-to-wear and the astronomical prices of Italian top designers, Zazù is a breath of fresh air. Transparent multilayered silk tunics inspired by the Japanese style, full skirts in shimmering silk, colorful cocktail dresses, well-cut jackets – and all at reasonable prices. Evening purses, embroidered or sequined, start from €70. Women with a taste for fashion will love it.

Malo

Calle delle Ostreghe, 2359, San Marco (Giglio)
☎ 041 523 21 62
Mon.-Sat. 9.30am-7.30pm, Sun. 10.30am-6.30pm.

If you are looking for a classic, high-quality, fine wool or cashmere sweater, you've come to the right place. Styling reminds one of the Jacky Kennedy era: overall, very conservative and very chic. Prices are high

(between €600 and €900), but the quality is irreproachable.

La Dogaressa

San Marco, 944 Calle Fiubera (Vallaresso)
☎ 041 241 19 84
Mon.-Sat. 10am-1pm and 3-7pm.

The choice in this ready-to-wear boutique is good: it goes from the very smart to the downscale. So you will find knitwear which is wonderfully figure-hugging and unstructured wear, "torn" or "ruffled" clothes, to satisfy the rebel in you. But everything is reasonable including the prices. Delightful welcome.

WHERE TO FIND THEM

All the big names in Italian haute couture and ready-to-wear clothes have branches near Piazza San Marco:
La Tour : calle larga S. Marco, 287, ☎ 041 522 51 47.
Missoni : calle Vallaresso, 1312/B, ☎ 041 520 57 33.
Gianni Versace : campo S. Moisè, 1462, ☎ 041 52 00 057.
La Perla : campo S. Salvador, 4828, ☎ 041 522 64 59.
Prada : Salizzada San Moisè, 1464, ☎ 041 528 39 66.
Max Mara : San Marco, 5033, Merceria dell'Orologio, ☎ 041 522 66 88

Children's treasures

Venice is teeming with small surprises for children: old-fashioned dolls, wooden tops, models of ships or gondolas, animal miniatures made of Murano glass, all made by craftsmen. If you have not brought the children with you, their eyes will light up with delight when you come back with all these treasures. For a little dress or a new baby gift browse in the many boutiques. Remember that in Italy the child is king!

Pettenello SAS

Campo S. Margherita, Dorsoduro, 2978
(Ca' Rezzonico)
☎ 041 523 11 67
Every day except Sun. (open during Carnival) 9.30am-1pm and 3.30-8pm.

An Aladdin's cave that will bring back childhood memories. You'll find all kinds of toys at all kinds of prices for your offspring, from kaleidoscopes to adorable music boxes, mobiles, pretty dolls and small reproductions of various objects (including *forcole*, gondola oar rests, and *brocole*, lagoon poles). You'll always be welcomed with a smile.

Amadi

San Polo, 2747, calle Saoneri
(San Tomà)
☎ 041 523 80 89
Mon.-Sat. 9.30am-1.30pm and 2.30pm-6.30pm; sometimes closed on Sat.

You see a lot of glass sculptures in the souvenir shops, completely expressionless and far removed from their originals. These are particularly well made because it is with the keen eye of the naturalist that Bruno Amadi, with his glass sticks, gives life to his little imaginary zoo. The birds from the lagoon start at €30 – the seagulls are incredibly lifelike. Butterflies (from €60), elephants, bustards, all realistic, simple but beautiful. Another shopwindow is filled with anchovies, sardines and vegetables, all in miniature.

Il Baule Blu

Calle del Mandolet, 2916/A, S. Tomà (S. Tomà)
☎ 041 71 94 48
Every day except Sun. 10.30am-12.30pm, 4-7.30pm.
Silvia and Claudia have a passion for toys. Old and new, whether in mint condition or in need of repair, they are all welcome here! You can find everything in this shop, from wooden toys to old toys made of tin and teddy bears from the thirties.

Emporio Il Nido delle Cigogne

Campo S. Tomà, 2806 (S. Tomà); ☎ 041 528 74 97
Every day except Sun. 9.30am-12.30pm, 3.30-7.30pm.

Everything you need to give your children a touch a Italian chic. Shoes and suits from Armani, Kenzo, Replay and many others.

La Scialuppa

Calle II° Saoneri, 2681 (S. Tomà)
☎ 041 719 372
Every day except Sun. 9.30am-12.30pm, 3-6pm (irregular opening hours).
Gilberto Gilberto Penzo builds wonderful scale models of ancient boats. The sea is his life's passion: He has written several books on the subject of boats and works at the Navy Museum. In his shop, you can buy scale models of gondolas in kit form, complete with instruction manuals. For children and grown-ups alike.

Ponte ai Giocattoli

Campiello Flaminio Corner, 5899 (Rialto)
Every day except Sun. 9am-12.30pm, 3.30-7.30pm.

Ask your way to the Ponte ai Giocattoli, "the bridge of toys." Next to the bridge, you'll find a small shop that sells an amazing collection of Barbie dolls: Barbie flamenco, Imperial Splendor, Butterfly and many others! These incredible collectors' items unfortunately fetch high prices: €250 to €340!

Dalla Venezia-Angelo

Calle Scalater, 2204 (S. Tomà)
☎ 041 72 16 59
Every day 8.30am-12.30pm and 3-8pm.
This is another good place to find unusual and original toys. Wood is king here and, with a little luck, you'll see the craftsman at work in his shop. The pretty tops would make good presents – they don't cost much and they're easy to pack.

TWO DAYS WITH THE CHILDREN

The Accademia gallery and Venetian gothic art will almost certainly leave the children cold, but they will definitely be interested in the arms room and old games room in the Correr Museum, or in the prisons of the Doges' Palace (tell them how Casanova escaped across the roofs), or even the dog cemetery in the Guggenheim Foundation. They can also go on a hunt for *trompe l'œil*, for example in the Gesuati Church.
Outdoors, apart from the change of scenery and ice creams galore, they will be intrigued by the funny leaning campaniles, soccer games on the *campi*, grimacing masks or the painted houses in Burano, or else by the *acqua alta* which changes Piazza San Marco into a giant puddle. Finally, note that water from the fountains is drinkable.

Leather accessories, chic accessories

No visit to Italy would be complete without the purchase of a pair of chic Italian shoes or a real leather (*vero cuoio*) wallet, belt or purse. A trip to Venice is no exception. Stylish, supple and beautifully made, Italian leather goods have a worldwide reputation. You may have to reach rather deep into your pockets, but it's an investment you won't regret that will probably last you a lifetime.

Gualti

Dorsoduro, 3111
Rio Terà Canal
(Ca' Rezzonico)
☎ 041 520 17 31
Mon.-Sat. 10am-1pm and 3-7.30pm.

At long last! The Dorsoduro is beginning to look like its crowd of aesthetes: a haunt for fashion designers. Gualti is one of them and designs his accessories like extensions of the body. His hair jewelry is like a moving sculpture, a mixture of resin and glass, very striking on top of a dark sheath dress (earrings start at €20). His woolen scarves (from €85), woven on a slightly rigid structure, seem to ripple as you wrap them over your shoulders. His pumps, made of silk satin (85 shades, two types of heels, €219) can be matched to the clutch bags, which are adorned with jewels. Everything is made on the premises.

Bruno Magli

Calle Vallaresso, 1302
(Vallaresso)
☎ 041 522 72 10
Mon.-Sat. 10.30am-7.30pm, Sun. 11.30am-6.30pm.

Anyone who likes traditional shoes should pay a visit to

this store, especially if they're men. The women's shoes, though elegant, are unadventurous.

La Bottega Veneta

Calle Vallaresso, 1337 (Vallaresso)
☎ 041 520 28 16
Mon.-Sat. 10am-7.30pm, Sun. 11am-7pm.

This *bottega* is an excellent place to find original, elegant purses and exclusive silk scarves. It specializes in braided leather for women, but is fairly expensive.

Fendi

S. Marco, 1474 (Vallaresso)
☎ 041 277 85 32
Mon.-Sat. 10am-7.30pm, Sun. 11am-1.30pm and 2.30-7pm.

Fendi clients are known to be willing to wait for months for the delivery of an item they have ordered. If accessories are not enough for you, Fendi also has a ready-to-wear line. Everything is beautiful and outrageously expensive: basic purses start at €1000, while a snake-skin model will cost €1700.

Barbieri 1945

Castello 3403, calle de la Madonna (S. Zaccaria)
☎ 041 522 81 77
Every day except Sun. 10am-12.30pm and 3.30-7.30pm.

Among the many high-quality accessories on sale in this shop, you'll find crumpled silk squares from €62, masses of elegant scarves and stoles, and silk ties from €55. The salespeople won't try to rush you because they know it can be very difficult to choose.

Ferragamo

Calle larga XXII Marzo, 2093 (Vallaresso)
☎ 041 277 85 09
Mon.-Sat. 10am-7pm, Sun. 11am-6pm.

It's worth stepping inside this boutique if only to admire the interior, wholly decorated in stone and chestnut panels. Obviously, while you're there, it would be a shame not to have a look at the shoes from the famous Florentine house, shoemakers to the stars.

Borsalino

Campo San Marco, 4822 (Vallaresso)
☎ 041 241 19 45
Mon.-Sat. 10am-1pm and 3.30-7.30pm.

The internationally famous makers of hats, with models and styles to suit everybody, from the classic Panama to the most eccentric beret. You're bound to find something that you like, if you're ready to pay the price. The boutique itself is highly original: sure to make your head spin!

Coccinelle

Mercerie San Marco, 4958 (Vallaresso)
☎ 041 277 06 58
Every day 10am-1pm and 3-7.30pm; closed Sunday in summer.

Coccinelle's purses, fine leathers, impeccable finish and fashionable styling have appealed to Italian women for many years. They've added accessories to their collections, and Coccinelle has become a lifestyle brand, offering both elegant and casual shoes, watches and jewelry.

And also...

Mori & Bozzi: Strada Nova, 2367/A ☎ 041 71 52 61.
Furla: Merceria San Salvador, 4833, S. Marco ☎ 041 277 04 60.
Glamour Calzature: Cannaregio, 1298, Ponte delle Guglie ☎ 041 71 62 46.

DANIELA GHEZZO SEGALIN A VENEZIA

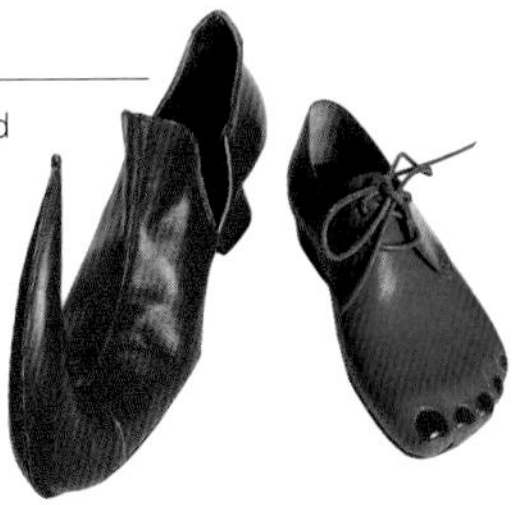

Totally unaffordable, and absolutely beautiful. Segalin's shoes are custom-made and will satisfy his clients' every whim, with eccentric styling and exquisite materials (such as ostrich and lizard skins). You can also have your shoes delivered.

Calle delle Fuseri, 4365, S. Marco (Rialto or Vallaresso)
☎ 041 522 21 15
Mon.-Sat. morning 9am-12.30pm and 3.30-7pm.

All that glitters

The Venetian goldsmiths have carved themselves an excellent reputation. All their creations are dazzlingly beautiful, but even the least costs an arm and a leg. If you can't afford one of these treasures, try looking in one of the souvenir shops instead. The Murano glass jewelry you can buy there – bracelets and necklaces – is adorable and equally typical of the city.

Nardi

Piazza S. Marco, 69 (Vallaresso)
☎ 041 523 21 50
Mon.-Sat. 10am-6.30pm in summer; Tue.-Sat. 9.30am-1pm and 3.30-7.30pm in winter.

This is the other great jewelry stores of Piazza San Marco besides Missiaglia. Among other pieces of jewelry, Nardi has created an *Othello* brooch encrusted with precious stones. You can also admire the elaborate work on the more affordable clocks, boxes, frames and compacts. Next to the Florian café.

Herriz

Calle larga XXII Marzo, 2381 (Vallaresso)
☎ 041 520 42 76
Tue.-Sat. 9.30am-12.30pm and 3-7pm.

This renowned antiques shop sells a vast range of antique jewelry made by famous names. Splashing out in this boutique is sure to be a real investment.

Chimento

Campo S. Moisè, 1460, S. Marco (Glglio)
☎ 041 523 60 10
Every day 10am-7.30pm; closed Sun.-Mon. in winter.

A jewelry store where you'll be able to find 18 carat gold that won't make a hole in your budget. Visit to see the zircon-encrusted pendants and the jewelry by Versace.

Bucintoro Arte

Merceria del Capitello, 4924 (Rialto)
☎ / Ⓕ 041 523 01 31
Every day 9.30am-7.30pm, Sun. 10.30am-7pm.

A dealer specializing in antique jewelry, whose shop you definitely should see if you're interested in buying some. His prices are only slightly higher than those of Attilio Codognato, his main competitor.

Missiaglia

Piazza S. Marco 125 (Vallaresso)
☎ 041 522 44 64
Mon.-Sat. 9.30am-12.30pm and 3.30-7.30pm.

A must – Missiaglia is none other than the appointed supplier to the great Venetian and Italian families since 1846. You really should go along to this jewelry store and goldsmith (at least to look at the treasures in the window) where you'll find objects to rival those of any other great city. Some exclusive items (lighters and necklaces in particular) are the work of highly talented Venetian artists. The store is next to the café Quadri (see p. 41).

Attombri

Sottoportico Orafi, 74, Rialto (Rialto)
☎ / Ⓕ 041 521 25 24
Mon.-Sat. 10am-1pm and 3-7pm.

The Attombri brothers create jewelry out of Murano glass. Their creations have already received considerable attention from the Italian fashion industry, starting with Romeo Gigli. Visit their tiny boutique near the Rialto to understand what all the fuss is about.

Attilio Codognato

Calle larga dell'Ascensione, 1295, San Marco (Vallaresso)
☎ 041 522 50 42
Tue.-Sat. 10am-1pm and 4-7pm.

If you only like antique jewelry, then this pretty shop is for you. You'll find here the widest possible choice of rings as well as cameos and a few contemporary pieces.

Sfriso

Campo S. Tomà, 2849 (S. Tomà)
☎ 041 522 35 58
Mon.-Sat. 9am-12.30pm and 3.30-7pm.

At Sfriso, every piece is unique and handcrafted with the tools of another age. The intimidating little shop in Campo S. Tomà houses all sorts of objects (ewers, dishes, cups, compacts, boxes and so on) made of gold or, more often, silver. The prices are astronomical, of course, but the name Sfriso is well-respected.

Antiquus

San Marco, 3131 Calle delle Botteghe (San Samuele)
☎ 041 520 63 95
Every day 10am-12.30pm and 3.30-7.30pm; closed Mon. morning.

This shop sparkles! In the smart street which joins the Campo Santo Stefano to the Grassi Palace where, among other things, you can find some contemporary art galleries, Antiquus offers Art Deco and 19th-century-style dinnerware and also silver jewelry set with gems or brilliants, brooches and drop earrings.

A LITTLE BIT OF FANTASY

Glass jewelry
This inexpensive jewelry is often made of colorful Murano glass. You'll find plenty of rings but even more bracelets and necklaces (starting at €3) in most of the glass shops in Venice and Murano (see pp. 114–115).

The jewelers of the Rialto
The Rialto Bridge is surrounded by a number of little stalls selling gold and silver jewelry – more fantasy than luxury – with something even for the smallest budget.

Velvet and silk

Venetian aristocrats buy from them when they wish to replace the hangings of their drawing rooms. The Italian State turns to them when it undertakes the renovation of a palace. These are well-established shops selling silk, Fortuny materials, velvet and Venice damask, though the atmosphere of the shops is rather hushed. Quality is faultless, and even if you do not redecorate your home, you can buy reasonably priced scarves and purses.

Mario Bevilacqua

Fondamenta Canonica, 337/B
(S. Zaccaria-3)
☎ 041 528 75 81
Every day 10am-7pm.

Opened in 1800, this boutique is in itself a real work of art: don't miss it! Movie buffs will enjoy looking at the stills from *Anonimo Veneziano*, a movie which was partly shot on the premises. The shop is a decorator's dream: fine cloth purses at €100 apiece. Mario Bevilacqua also has another boutique in Venice, on Campo Santa Maria Giglio, 2520, ☎ 041 241 06 62.

Emma Gaggio

Campo S. Stefano, 3441
(S. Samuele)
☎ 041 522 85 74
Mon.-Sat. morning 10.30am-1pm and 4-7pm.

A well-known store in calle delle Botteghe, specializing in silk and printed velvet, taking inspiration from Art Deco drawings and Fortuny designs (see p. 16). You'll also find accessories (stoles, slippers) and cushions. The entrance is charming.

Lorenzo Rubelli

Palazzo Corner-Spinelli
S. Angelo, 3877
(S. Angelo)
☎ 041 523 61 10
Every day except Sun. 9.30am-12.30pm and 3.30-7pm.

This shop is an institution that produces tiny amounts

of sumptuous handwoven damask and velvet. Its extraordinary handstamped velvet is used to decorate Venetian palaces.

Vittorio Trois

Campo S. Maurizio, 2666 (Giglio)
☎ 041 522 29 05
Mon.-Sat. 10am-1pm and 4-7.30pm.

The only place in Venice where you can buy the famous Fortuny fabrics. But at €238 a meter/yard, you risk ruin if you want to turn your home into a Venetian palace.

Venetia Studium

Via XXII Marzo, 2425 (workshop) or Mercerie, 723 (S. Zaccaria or Rialto) and S. Marco, 2403 (Giglio) (shops)
☎ 041 522 92 81
F 041 522 73 53
Every day 9.30am-7.40pm, Sun. 10.30am-6pm.

More Fortuny-inspired silk and velvet. The price of the scarves, which are absolutely gorgeous, starts at €145 and goes sky-high. The Fortuny lamps are fantastic and there are pretty purses for around €75. You can visit the workshops if you like.

Valeria Bellinaso

Campo S. Aponal, 1226 (S. Silvestro)
☎ 041 522 33 51
Mon.-Sat. 10am-1.30pm and 3.30-7.30pm, Sun. 11am-1pm and 4-7pm; closed Sun.Jan.-Mar. and Jul.-Aug.

In Valeria's shop, you can easily get lost among all the silk and velvet stoles, hats, scarves, sunvisors and shoes. The designs, which are all original, are made exclusively for the shop by craftsmen. You'll be surprised by the interesting and unusual combinations of colors. Costs between €90 and €300 for a hat and between €100 and €120 for a scarf.

Pasinetti

Campiello Ca' Bernardi, 1321 (S. Silvestro)
☎ 041 522 32 65
F 041 522 88 21
Mon.-Fri. 9am-noon, 3-6pm.

The illustrious house of Pasinetti, which is housed in the Palazzo Bernardi, sells fabrics of breathtaking beauty.

QUICK GUIDE

- Brocade: embossed silk fabric, often containing a large amount of gold and silver thread.
- Damask: silk fabric with the same pattern appearing on the right side (in satin on a taffeta background) and the wrong side (in taffeta on a satin background).
- Taffeta: silk with a plain weave.
- Artificial and natural silk: When it comes in contact with fire, natural silk burns slowly without flames. Artificial silk flares up and is quickly consumed by fire.
- Care of velvet: Velvet loses its sheen with wear. You can restore its suppleness by wetting it on the wrong side and holding it over a hot iron (being careful not to let them touch), then leaving it to dry in the air.

Masks
at the ready!

There are countless Carnival shops, maybe too many. To differentiate themselves from those who mass-produce soulless masks, the best Venetian craftsmen play the creative card. They rack their brains to invent ever new models because there's nothing worse than going to the Carnival in the same costume as your neighbor!

Il Sole e la Luna

Frezzeria, 1232
(Vallaresso)
☎ 041 523 38 51
Ⓕ 041 528 75 43
Every day 10am-8pm
(10am-11pm May-Nov.)

This boutique brings together the works of some of the best traditional Venetian craftsmen and artists. Here, you will find masks, costumes, collectors' puppets and other handmade artifacts. If you're lucky, you might even be shown around this treasure trove by Antonia Sautter herself, the creator and owner of this shop worthy of Ali Baba.

Mondonovo Maschere

Di Lovato Guerrino, 3063, Dorsoduro
(Ca' Rezzonico)
☎ 041 528 73 44
Mon.-Sat. 9am-6.30pm.

This is where the artists of the Commedia dell'Arte theater come to order their masks. The shop and workshop near Campo S. Margherita is worth more than a quick visit. You'll find more than 300 masks here, at a wide range of prices and to suit all tastes.

La Bottega d'Arte-Il Cignoca

Calle limeto la Sacrestia, 4361 (S. Zaccaria)
☎ 041 590 61 71
Every day 11am-7pm.

You'll find masks at very good prices in this shop near Piazza San Marco, especially gilded masks for under €30. There's plenty of choice of both papier-mâché and leather masks. If you are interested, the craftsman will explain the various steps involved in making the masks.

Papier-mâché

Calle lunga S. M. Formosa, 5175, Castello (Rialto)
☎ 041 522 99 95
Mon.-Sat. 9am-7.30pm, Sun. 10am-7pm.

This elegant shop, resembling an art gallery, sells not only very ornate masks but also beautiful handpainted ceramics. Everything is attractively priced and the salespeople will offer you good advice.

Balocoloc

Calle longa, S. Croce (S. Stae)
☎ / Ⓕ 041 524 05 51
Tue.-Sat. 9am-6pm.

If you're looking for the costume that'll make you a star of the Carnival, Balocoloc is a must. Great clothes, masks and cocked hats at reasonable prices.

La Venexiana Atelier

Castello, 4322, ponte della Canonica (San Zaccaria)
☎ 041 523 35 58
Every day 10.30am-7pm (10.30pm in summer).

A very pleasant shop that's worth a look in itself, with an excellent craftsman specializing in traditional handpainted papier-mâché masks. La Venexiana Atelier also has Carnival clothes and pretty, old-fashioned dolls. There's another shop in San Marco (☎ 041 528 68 88, same hours), or at 1135/A, on Frezzeria.

L'Arlecchino

San Polo, 789, ruga vecchia San Giovanni (San Silvestro)
☎ 041 520 82 20
Mon.-Sat. 9.30am-7.30pm; sometimes open Sun.

One of the best selections of masks in Venice. Also more affordable papier-mâché masks (from around €16), costumes and loads of souvenirs are on sale here.

Atelier Pietro Longhi

Campo dei Frari, 2604/B, San Polo (S. Tomà)
☎ 041 71 44 78
www.pietrolonghi.com
Every day except Sat. 9am-1pm and 2.30-7.30pm.

If you feel like buying or renting a theater or opera costume, Petro Longhi is the man for you. Go there at least to admire this fabulous shop. If you don't find a costume, you can always opt for a gondolier hat for about €30.

Tragicomica

San Tomà, 2800, San Polo (S. Tomà)
☎ / Ⓕ 041 72 11 02
www.tragicomica.it
Every day 10am-7pm (6pm Sun.).

If you like rummaging amongst piles of clutter, then this is the shop for you. You can stumble across superb wooden puppets (Pinocchio costs €520), and pretty dolls and masks from €29. Opposite Goldoni's house.

A WORD OF ADVICE

It's better to buy from craftsmen displaying *artigiano veneziano* stickers in their windows, as they make the masks from start to finish. Other shops either buy in white masks that are then painted by workers or simply sell masks bought in batches. Taking into account the markup of the shops, you may find you'll pay more for a good mask if you buy in ordinary shops than if you buy from craftsmen, or you may end up with a mass-produced mask. You will find authentic craftsmen at the addresses shown here.

Murano glassware

If it's not a mask, it'll be a piece of Murano glassware that you take back from your weekend in Venice. The shops number in the hundreds! To avoid buying mass-produced glass or Murano-style imports, it's better to visit the museum first to develop a practised eye, then visit the workshops on the island or the showrooms in Piazza San Marco. After that you'll be ready to take your pick.

Battiston

Calle Vallaresso, 1320 (Vallaresso).
☎ 041 523 05 09
Every day 9.30am-7.30pm (11pm weekends in summer).

One of the main places to buy Murano glass in Venice. There are very beautiful blue glass dishes, pretty colored bottles that are more affordable (around €50 according to size) and, lastly, the well-known stylish carafes from Harry's Bar (which is just next door) that will look very chic on your table at home.

Galerie Rossella Junck

Calle delle Ostreghe, 2360 (Giglio); ☎ 041 520 77 47
San Marco 1997, Campo San Fantin (Giglio)
☎ 041 521 07 59
www.rossellajunck.it
Mon.-Sat. 10am-12.30pm, 3.30-7.30pm.

Dedicated to the contemporary glass creations of young artists from all over Europe, the two galleries of Turinese Rossella Junck have given a new vitality to Murano's traditional glass industry. Contemporary works are exhibited in the gallery on calle delle Ostreghe – as for her gallery on Campo San Fantin, it contains a beautiful collection of 18th-century glassworks. Whichever shop you visit, you won't be disappointed.

Venini

Piazzetta dei Leoncini, 314 (S. Zaccaria)
☎ 041 522 40 45; Every day except Sun. 9.30am-7.30pm.

A famous shop and one of the ten most important around Piazza San Marco. It'll give you a good idea of what the best contemporary designers are producing.

On Murano

Domus Vetri d'Arte

Fondamenta Vetrai, 82
☎ / Ⓕ 041 73 92 15
Every day 9am-6pm (5pm Sun.).

A shop very different from the stalls on the *fondamente* of Murano. An ashtray/dish may cost around €85, but it's by Ercole Moretti, one of the best designers around. The warm welcome and personal service come as a bonus.

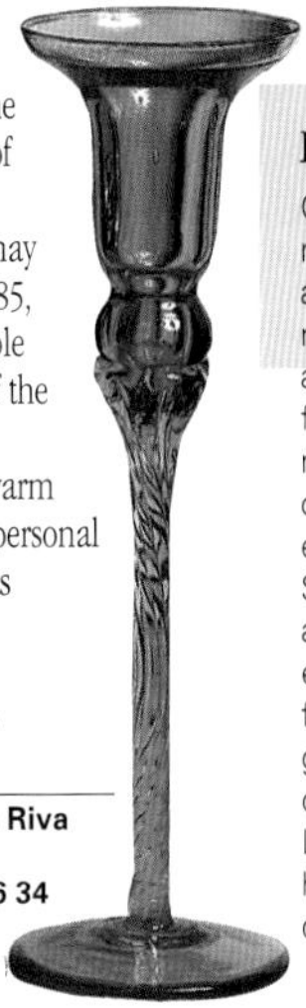

Artstudio Murano

Fondamenta Riva Longa, 48
☎ 041 527 46 34
9.30am-5.30pm.

Here, young craftsmen make contemporary jewelry out of Murano glass. You might be interested to know that they also offer courses in jewelry-making. Necklaces costs €21 to €48 – highly original gifts at affordable prices.

Barovier & Toso

Fondamenta Vetrai, 28
☎ 041 73 90 49
www.barovier.com
Showroom: Every day except Sun. morning 10am-1pm and 2-5.30pm.

This museum was created in 1995, and set up in the Contarini Palace in Murano.
Exhibited permanently are 250 objects from the Barovier & Toso collection. Guided visits, Monday to Friday, between 10 and 11am, and between 3 and 4pm. You can also book a private visit by calling ☎ 041 73 90 49 to make an appointment. In the showroom, you can purchase works from some of Italy's greatest designers (from €250 to more than €1000).

More worthwhile addresses...

Find more master craftsmen at the following addresses:
Carlo Moretti: Fond. Manin, 3/13, Murano ☎ 041 73 62 72.
Archimede Seguso: Fond. Serenella, 18, Murano ☎ 041 73 90 48.
Gino Cenedese: Piazza S. Marco, 40 ☎ 041 522 54 87.
Massimo Micheluzzi: Dorsoduro 1071, Ponte delle Maravegie; ☎ 041 528 21 90.
Bottega d'Angolo: San Marco 803, calle Fiubera ☎ 041 523 52 37.
And also **Mazzega** (see p. 69).

HINTS ON BUYING MURANO

Go directly to Murano if you wish to renew your collection of glass candies, they are cheaper on the island (€1or €2 each). For a more important purchase, the best piece of advice we can give is never buy anything in the first shop you come across, unless you really fall in love with something, of course. Another precaution is to examine the glass carefully on all sides. Some "Murano" glass turns out to be a cheap copy from southeast Asia. Be extra careful if the price is low and feel its weight in your hand – good Murano glass must be heavy and should sound like crystal does when you flick it with a fingernail. Lastly, the glass shops, especially those on Murano, have rather flexible opening hours. In summer and during the Carnival, most are open on Sunday and until fairly late at night.

Lace and household linen

Once again, Venice won't fail to amaze you. These shops offer all kinds of bed and table linen and nightgowns, not to mention the main Venetian speciality, *merletti*, the lace once made by the women of Burano while their fishermen husbands were away at sea. You may still see some of the women today on the thresholds of their brightly colored houses, making the intricate lace used to decorate tablecloths, napkins and blouses.

Jesurum

Merceria del Capitello, 4857 (Vallaresso)
☎ 041 520 61 77
Mon.-Sat. 9.30am-7.30pm, Sun. 10.30am-6.30pm.

You'll find this extraordinary showroom behind the basilica in the former Scuola S. Apollonia, a veritable monument to the splendor of the large trading companies. Here you can admire or buy not only the finest lace in Venice but also household linen and ladies' fashions. Here, too, you'll see tables set with exquisite tableware that will make you truly envious. Jesurum is unquestionably the best place to buy table linen and lace. Their prices may be high, but you can find tablecloths that will impress your guests for as little as €120 or €160 – or even less during the January and July clearance sales.

Capricci e Vanità

Dorsoduro, 3744, calle San Pantalon (S. Tomà)
☎ 041 523 15 04

Every day 10am-12.30pm and 4-7.30pm; closed Mon. morning and Sun.

The shopwindow displays dresses and woollen pullovers, cardigans within everyone's pocket (€95) and shawls worth €125. Yet the two dressmakers who are here mainly work with lace making nightgowns and household linen. Venetian women know this address well. You are attended to with a smile.

Anniele Pizzi e ricami

Calle lunga San Barnaba, 2748
(Ca' Rezzonico)
☎ 041 520 32 77
Mon.-Sat. morning 9.30am-12.30pm and 4-7.30pm.

Hidden in an alleyway, this small boutique offers embroidered nightgowns, bed linen, cotton and linen dresses for children which can be custom-made. Less expensive, pretty bags for your lingerie (around €10) or for lavender, and charming little boxes made of embroidered linen, €4 each.

La Fenice Atelier

San Marco, 3537
Calle dei Frati
(S. Angelo)
☎ 041 523 05 78
Every day 10.30am-7.30pm (11am Sun.).

The third generation is in control of this remarkable shop selling lingerie and household linen, open at this address since 1995 (the first one was located just next to La Fenice, hence its name). The bathrobes and the nightgowns (from €90 made of cotton, €250 in silk) are altered to your size. Very romantic cuts. Place mats €18 apiece made of cotton, €28 in linen. There also tablecloths, sheets and charming pillowcases trimmed with lace. Some articles are handmade.

On Burano

Emilia

Piazza Galuppi, 205-207
☎ 041 73 52 45
Every day 9.30am-6pm.

The biggest lace shop on the island, if not the best. It stocks an incomparable selection of tablecloths and napkins, clothes, handkerchiefs and doilies of all sizes at all prices (from as little as €6). The charming salespeople will be happy to advise you. There's also a small museum.

Martina, merletti d'Arte

Via S. Mauro, 307 and 337
☎ 041 73 55 23
Every day 9.30am-6pm
Closed for a week in January.

Rather than looking at the household linen, quite classic on the whole, cast a glance at the lace blouses, the crossover tops and the embroidered bustiers from €49. It is a feminine style that will suit you if you like fine embroideries and wide frills.

BEFORE BUYING LACE...

Pay a visit to the lace museum in Burano to see the best there is in the way of Venetian *merletto*. Then go and visit the shops on the island keeping a cool head. If the price of a sizable piece of lace is tempting, you're more than likely to be looking at something made in Taiwan. Before you buy a piece, look it over very carefully and find out where it was made.

Art Deco interiors

The great international design brands are located between the San Lio and San Marina campi, near the Rialto. Here you can also discover the quite exceptional wooden pieces by Livio de Marchi, A Mano lighting (100 percent Venetian) and stores selling handpainted ceramics. When it comes to table art, European design – and above all Italian – is second to none!

Margherita Ceramiche

Sottoportigo della Siora Bettina (between calle della Regina and Campo S. Cassiano), 2345 (S. Stae)
☎ 041 72 31 20
Mon.-Sat. morning 10am-7pm.

Yellow and blue ceramics with floral motifs that will brighten up your table without ruining you. There are two styles of dishes, with prices starting at €20 for the smallest. Why pay more when here the ceramics are all handpainted?

A Mano

San Polo, 2616, rio Terrà (San Tomà)
☎ 041 71 57 42
Every day 10am-1.30pm and 2.30-7.30pm.

The aerial sculptures first attract the eye, then one discovers items made of different metals, such as lighting effects in bronze.

Some of them look like mobiles by Calder. Others evoke a simple flower or a totem. The artist Alessandro Salvadori makes lamps on site. A mixture of influences, via Japan, Africa and elsewhere to join up again in Venice. Prices start from €135, €40 for a frame. Jewelry is also available. Near the Campo dei Frari.

Madera

Dorsoduro, 2762, Campo San Barnaba (Ca' Rezzonico)
☎ 041 522 41 81
Mon.-Sat. 10.30am-1pm and 3.30-7.30pm.

Contemporary chic table art was beginning to be cruelly lacking in Venice. In this red and white boutique there is a selection of two-tone ceramic German bowls for €12, delightful porcelain lamps by Stephanie Hering, handmade ceramics by Alfredo Gioventu and, also German, Blomus with his coffee measure (€10) or, ultra-lovely, his metal cutting-spoon for eating a kiwi fruit with false modesty (€12).

Planet Earth

Dorsoduro, 3002, Campo Santa Margherita (Ca' Rezzonico)
☎ 041 528 67 00
Every day 10am-1pm and 3-7.30pm.

At the edge of Santa Margherita Square, this boutique of objets d'art is just as international as the crowd which haunts the campo day and night. The trendy young Venetians don't miss a scrap of current trends for "home sweet home": zen candles, raku table services, cushions in brilliant velvet, wrought-iron shelves... Does this remind you of something? A concept store of ethnic Oriental character.

Rigattieri

Calle dei Frati, 3532-3536, S. Marco (S. Angelo)
☎ 041 523 10 81
Every day except Sun. and Mon. morning. 9am-1pm and 3-7pm.

The best choice of tableware made in Bassano, a small town in the interior of the country specializing in the production of handpainted ceramics that sell for a correspondingly high price. The shopwindow full of vases, tureens, eggs and animals is amazing.

Livio de Marchi

Salizzada S. Samuele, 3157/A, S. Marco (S. Samuele)
☎ 041 528 56 94
Mon.-Fri. 9am-12.30pm and 1.30-6pm.

The only shop and workshop of its kind in Venice, where you can find the designs of Livio de Marchi, including socks, shirts, ties and a variety of other objects made of wood. The prices vary, but there are some affordable pieces.

In addition...

Don't forget the glass vases by Murano, coasters or lace napkins by Burano, Fortuny lamps. There is no shortage of ideas in the other boutiques we have selected.

ALESSI AND BIALETTI

You won't necessarily find a bargain shopping here, but it is terribly snobbish! Among the range of "useful souvenirs" is first and foremost Alessi. La Bottega dell'Acciaio, an adorable micro-boutique in Fiubera Street (San Marco, 791, ☎ 041 522 85 09) is packed with Alessi! Here you will find everything it is possible to have in this brand. And why not bring back a Bialetti cafetiere (there is a wider choice than elsewhere)? Past the Ratti drugstore, at the foot of the San Lio salizzada (Castello, 5825, ☎ 041 260 46 00), or Epicentro, calle dei Fabbri (San Marco, 932, ☎ 041 522 68 64).

The art of paper in Venice

If you want to take home a typically Venetian souvenir that's both chic and fairly inexpensive, stationery is ideal. Just step inside one of the many tiny *legatorie* of the Serenissima and you'll find stationery of every kind – and can also watch real craftsmen at work, perhaps recalling childhood memories of the smell of paper and ink.

Linda Maria Gonzalez

Calle del Sruttariol, 1854 (Giglio)
☎ 041 528 55 63
Every day 10am-7.30pm.

A local craftsman offers a wide variety of stationery products, including classic letter paper and a large number of datebooks and address books bound in imitation panther and zebra (around €15). Worth a look, even if only for the shopwindow.

Paolo Olbi

Calle del Mandola, 3653 (S. Angelo)
☎ 041 528 50 25
Every day except Mon. morning, 10am-7.30pm; Sep.-Oct. 11am-7.30pm.

A *legatoria* where you'll find pencils, leather-bound datebooks, photograph albums and sketchpads covered in marbled paper. You can also have a stamp made with the design of your choice for a very reasonable price.

Il Papiro

Calle del Piovan, 2764 (Giglio)
☎ 041 522 30 55
Every day 10am-7.30pm (10.30am Sun.).

Datebooks and other notebooks covered in marbled paper, as well as more original stationery for young and old alike, all at affordable prices, including pens, seals, colored pencils and very attractive greeting cards.

Alberto Valese

Campo S. Stefano, 3471 (S. Angelo or S. Samuele)
☎ 041 523 88 30
Mon.-Sat. 10am-1pm and 2.30-7pm, Sun. 11am-6pm.

Along with the Legatoria Piazzesi, this is the other great marbled paper specialist you really mustn't miss. Alberto

Valese reproduces his original patterns on a multitude of objects, including notebooks, boxes and small papier-mâché drawers, as well as silk and crêpe de Chine scarves. You may see one of his workers making floral prints using special techniques in the back room.

Karisma

Salizzada San Polo, 2752/A (S. Tomà)
☎ 041 71 06 70
Every day 9.30am-7.30pm.

Located in a small alley near the Casa Goldoni, this little stationery shop sells the products of local Venetian craftsmen. As in most of the town's stationery shops, you'll find Murano glass fountain pens and other classics, but Karisma also sells some highly original products, such as lovely cotton paper datebooks (between €12 and €20) and distinctive leather-bound notepads (between €24 and €60), all of which are handmade.

Legatoria Piazzesi

Campo S. M. del Giglio, 2511/C (Giglio)
☎ 041 522 12 02
Every day except Sun. 10am-1pm and 4-7pm.
Make a visit to the oldest *legatoria* in Venice a matter of priority, even though the prices are high. It's a marvelous shop with an endless variety of original binding paper and expensive but gorgeous boxes covered in marbled paper, as well as chutes and ladders sets, playing cards, tarot cards and papier-mâché Commedia dell'Arte figurines.

Legatoria Polliero

Campo dei Frari, 2995 (S. Tomà)
☎ 041 528 51 30
Mon.-Sat. 10am-1pm and 4-7.30pm, Sun. 10am-1pm.
This tiny *legatoria* in the shadow of the gigantic church of the Frari has marvelous marbled-paper objects, from small pocket datebooks to large desk appointment books. You may be able to have your favorite small book bound for at least €65 and you can even have it sent home.

Gianni Basso

Calle del Fumo, 5306, Cannaregio (Fondamente Nuove)
☎ 041 523 46 81
Mon.-Sat. morning 8.30am-12.30pm and 2-6.30pm.

You must seek it out, this tiny shop-cum-workshop of the *stampatore* (printer) Gianni Basso. In this irresistible place filled with the smell of ink, you can choose the logo to put on your business card just like the Labecque sisters and Hugh Grant, the actor, before you. The prices depend on the order.

THE *LEGATORIE*

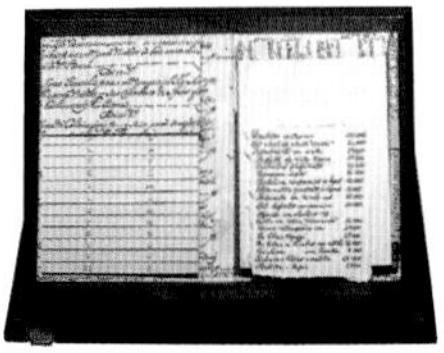

The word *legatoria* originally designated a bookbinding workshop (from *legato*, meaning "bound"), but in the end bookbinding gave way to the manufacture of notebooks covered in marbled paper (all sizes) and stationery in the broader sense of the term (ink, seals, etc.). You can rummage around at will here and ask the craftsmen for advice if you can't find what you're looking for at the right price (from €5 for a small notebook and around €20 for a 10cm x 15cm (4in x 6in) notebook with about 70 pages, which is better value for money). There are good reductions to be had in the New Year sales.

Books
and music

If you like fine books or reproductions of old prints, you won't be disappointed. Venice has a large number of bookstores whose shelves are literally collapsing under the weight of art books, sometimes at bargain prices.

Bertoni

Calle de la Mandola, 3637/B (S. Angelo); ☎ 041 522 95 83
Every day except Sun. and Aug. 9am-12.45pm and 3.30-7.30pm.

A family run bookstore that's been handed down from father to son. It has new, old and secondhand books on art and architecture. You have to rummage around, but you can usually find something of interest.

Fantoni Libri

Salizzada S. Luca, 4119 (Rialto)
☎ 041 522 07 00
Every day except Sun. 10am-2pm, 4-8pm.

A bookstore you shouldn't miss if you like fine books and art books or are interested in architecture and design. It also has a selection of reviews (in Italian) that will fascinate fans of architecture and the graphic arts.

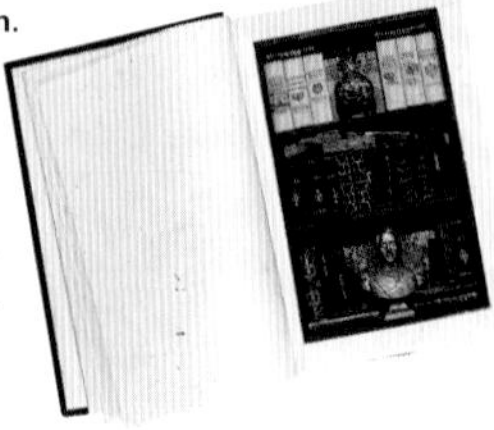

Filippi

Calle del Paradiso, 5763 (Rialto)
☎ 041 523 56 35
Every day 9am-12.30pm and 3.30-7.30pm.

A publishing house and bookstore without rival for everything to do with the Serenissima. If there's a work (old or new) on any aspect of the history or culture of Venice, you're almost certain to find it here. They also have a collection of fine reproductions of old prints at affordable prices.

Linea d'Acqua

San Marco, 3717/A (S. Angelo)
☎ 041 522 40 30
Mon.-Sat. 10am-1pm and 3.30-7pm.

Nearly at the foot of the Ponte de la Cortesia, before the Campo Manin, Linea d'Acqua is a general bookstore (novels, art) with an excellent choice of books about Venice. Less comprehensive choice than some others, but it is in the center.

Goldoni

Calle dei Fabbri, 4742 (Rialto)
☎ 041 522 23 84
Mon.-Sat. 9.30am-7.30pm.

An excellent general bookstore with a fine choice of guides. For quite a considerable amount, you can

buy a facsimile that will make your friends green with envy – nine long plates of all the houses on the Grand Canal. It's a faithful reproduction of the 1828 work owned by the Biblioteca Marciana.

Toletta

Sacca della Toletta, 1213 (Ca' Rezzonico or Accademia)
☎ 041 523 20 34
Mon.-Sat. 9.30am-1pm and 3.30-7.30pm in summer;

Mon.-Sat. 9.30am-6.30pm, Sun. 3-7.30pm in winter.
The place in Venice to buy new and secondhand art books at reduced prices (up to 50 percent off). According to those in the know, there's nowhere else like it in Italy.

Giovanni e Paolo

Campo SS. Giovanni e Paolo, 6358 (Ospedale)
☎ 041 522 96 59
Every day except Sun. 9am-12.30 pm and 3.30-7.30pm.

Whatever type of literature concerning the Serenissisma that you may have wished to read in your hotel, and have forgotten to bring with you on your travels, this bookstore has them all. Emphasis on French books. Francophiles are particularly welcome!

VENETIAN MUSIC VIVALDI STORE

Opposite the post office (Fontego dei Tedeschi), the Vivaldi Store is entirely dedicated to Venetian Renaissance music (Gabrieli, Monteverdi, Vivaldi) and baroque music (Albinoni, Marcello). Listening to *The Four Seasons* in the very town Vivaldi lived may sound very different; this specialist store also offers, under the label "Nalesso Record," recordings of several concerts played in Venice from the original scores. Moreover, Vivaldi Store can reserve (for a fee) your seats for concerts (churches, La Fenice, theaters, etc.).

San Marco, 5537-5540, Campo San Bartolomeo (Rialto)
☎ 041 522 13 43
Mon.-Sat. 9.30am-7.30pm, Sun. 11am-7pm.

Antiques and secondhand goods

You won't have a problem finding the main antiques dealers – they're all concentrated around La Fenice and Campo S. M. del Giglio. The Baroque gilded frames, antique furniture, Rococo painted panels and 19th-century paintings are all highly desirable, but cost a small fortune. Only the books and the traditional glassware decorated with a thin gold line won't make too much of a dent in your savings, although it all depends on their age.

Fabris Giulia Antichità

Campo S. Maurizio, 2606 (Giglio); ☎ 041 523 70 54

Every day except Sun. 10am-1pm and 3.30-7pm.

An interesting antiques dealer who searches the attics of Venetian residences for rare items of furniture and old objects. It's easy to imagine the marvels he finds there. The stock often changes.

Beppe Patitucci

Campo S. M. del Giglio, 2511/B (Giglio); ☎ 041 522 12 02 Mon.-Sat. 11am-1pm, 3-7pm.

Apart from millionaires, only those fond of old books will have any hope of buying anything in Beppe Patitucci's very smart shop. The rest will look with envy at the magnificent gilded wood furniture and doors painted with Rococo motifs.

Antichità Zancopé Vetri

Campo S. Maurizio, 2674 (Giglio)
☎ 041 523 45 67
Mon.-Sat. 10am-1pm and 4.30-7.30pm.

The house of Guiditta I Zancope has been outwitting all its competitors since 1838. Among the items on display in the shop are old paintings, 19th-century prints, telescopes, retorts and, above all, an incomparable choice of 16th- to 18th-century Venetian glassware, the specialty of this top-quality shop.

Francisco Saverio Mirate

Calle della Verona, 1904 (Giglio)
☎ 041 522 76 00
Mon.-Sat. 10am-12pm and 4-7pm.

Another antiques shop for you to feast your eyes on, housed in an old Venetian residence, itself worth going out of your way to see. Paintings in gilded period frames (mainly

19th century), elaborately shaped mirrors and painted wooden furniture, sometimes decorated with trompe l'œil motifs.

Gian Paolo Tolotti

Calle del Forno, 42/48, Cannaregio (Ca' d'Oro)
☎ 041 528 52 62
Every day except Sun. 9am-12pm and 4-7pm.

One of the major names in top-quality antiques, with a vast choice of beautiful objects on offer, including old prints, lamp bases, lanterns and more affordable small silver objects.

La Luna nel Pozzo

Calle lunga S. Barnaba, 2860 (Ca' Rezzonico)
☎ 041 523 70 72
Every day except Sun. 10.30am-1pm and 4-7.30pm.

For the last 30 years, this antiques dealer has been restoring furniture from old Venetian houses and farther afield, from the rest of Italy. He also has a selection of early 19th-century English furniture, Murano vases from the thirties and antique jewelry.

Totem-Il Canale

Rio Terrà A. Foscarini, 878/B (Accademia)
☎ 041 522 36 41.
Every day except Sun. 10am-1pm and 3-7pm.

An African art gallery which dedicates some space to jewels made of *antiche perle veneziane* (ancient Venetian beads). Take advantage of the particularly reasonable prices.

A. BARUTTI LACADOR

Alfredo Barutti, in his ageless shop on the Campo Manin, has little interest in fame. Go and watch him restore furniture and gilded wooden frames, and especially the fabulous Art Deco models he sells for a considerable amount.

Campo Manin, 4231, S. Marco (S. Angelo or Rialto)
☎ 041 528 73 16
Every day except Sun. 8.30am-12.30pm and 3.30-7.30pm (inquire before visiting).

Eating and drinking

Venetian grocers may turn out to be your downfall. From the side of the *calle*, they'll offer you a multitude of tempting, inexpensive specialties – pasta of every color, fragrant oil and vinegar, good, strong coffee, bottles of Prosecco and aperitifs, and the San Daniele ham that's said to be tastier than that of neighboring Parma. All these *etti* (1 *etto* = 100g/3 1/2oz) and bottles may add a lot of extra weight to your luggage.

Pastificio Giacomo Rizzo

Salizzada S. Giovanni Crisostomo, 5778, Cannaregio (Rialto)
☎ 041 522 28 24
Every day except Sun. and Wed. 8.30am-1pm and 3.30-7.30pm.

Traditional handmade pasta made with garlic or curry, as well as blue curaçao, dark chocolate and bilberries, but definitely no added food colors. Also *miele amaro di corbezzolo* (bitter arbutus honey) and an amazing variety of olive oils and vinegars (with garlic, basil, lemon, chilies, etc.).

Latteria De Grandis and Sinigaglia

Calle del Mondo Nuovo, 5793/A, Castello (Rialto)
☎ 041 522 80 62
Every day except Sun. 7.30am-1pm and 4.30-7.30pm.

Probably the best choice of hams, sausages and

cheeses in the city (and all from Venetia). A good place to buy San Daniele ham at a very reasonable price.

Luciano Mascari

Ruga degli Speziali, 381, S. Polo
(Rialto)
☎ 041 522 97 62
Every day except Sun. and Wed. 8am-1pm and 4-7.30pm.

As well as coffees with heady aromas, one of the best coffee merchants in Venice offers a ridiculous choice of inexpensive herbal teas and candies. The *gianduja* (hazelnut cream with chocolate) in a jar (around €4) is enough to make you swoon with happiness. Also see the wine merchant **Cantina ai Mori** (see p. 65).

Rialto market

Rialto
Market every day except Sun. and Mon. (fish market only) 8am-12pm.

Come here on Saturday from 11am to noon, when it's in full swing. A few places to look out for are the delicatessen at no. 214, the cheesemonger, Sbrissa, at nos. 88–90 and the fresh pasta shop at no. 219 (five or six different sorts of gnocchi).

Casa della Grappa

Ruga Rialto, 779/A, S. Polo
(Rialto or S. Silvestro)
☎ 041 523 65 78
Every day 9.30am-7.30pm.

This is the home of grappa. You'll find it here in all its forms (Prosecco grappa, Valpolicella grappa, etc.), and the narrower the bottle, the higher the price – not that the shape of the bottle matters. Also stocks wine and pasta.

Bottigleria Colonna

Calle della Fava, 5595, Castello
(Rialto)
☎ and Ⓕ 041 528 51 37
Every day except Sun. 9am-1pm and 4-8pm.

A wine shop that sells tasting packs with from three up to a dozen different vintages from Venetia or Lombardy, all for the price of Beaujolais Nouveau or little more. Ideal for getting to know all the varieties of Prosecco. Also a wide choice of Italian aperitif wines.

WHERE TO FIND GROCERY STORES

Forget the area around Piazza S. Marco and S. Lucia station, where the grocers fleece foreigners without even a smile. Shop where the Venetians shop, on the other side of the Rialto, in Cannaregio (Strada Nova and Rio Terrà S. Leonardo) or Castello (Via G. Garibaldi and around Campo S. M. della Fava). There are also the Standa shops (open every day except Sun. 8.30am-7.20pm), the local supermarkets in Campo S. Luca (S. Marco) or, better still, Strada Nova, near Campo S. Felice.

Practicalities

Musical life is intense in Venice, but only if you like classical music because it's fair to say that the other types are not so well represented. Nevertheless Venice has its wine or beer bars and choice places to start an evening out, together with discos and its casinos to end it. All the same, you'll probably go to bed early.

Finding out

You can read in the specialized column of the two daily newspapers *Il Gazzettino* and *La Nuova Venezia* details of the concerts of the day, cabarets in the night bars, and disco parties (mainly in the Lido and Mestre).

In *Un ospite di Venezia* (a free weekly available nearly everywhere, and in the tourist information center), you will be able to see all the shows that are on (locations and times), the concerts of the week in the churches, cultural events and practical information about the city. Also on www.unospitedivenezia.it. *Leo Bussola* (a free brochure, available in the tourist information center, at the airport and in some hotels) is published every other month and gives more or less the same information as *Un ospite di Venezia*, with a classification day by day and a map of the *vaporetto*. Also available on www.hellovenezia.it. *Venezia da vivere*, a free bilingual quarterly at the tourist information center, is very good (and very well produced) for nights out, to choose a bar, go for a drink in an "in" place, have a late bite or dance. Also available on www.veneziadavivere.com. Another two sites list the

THE GRAND CANAL BY NIGHT

A boat ride on the Grand Canal at night shouldn't be missed. The most beautiful "street" in the world is a magical sight. You can see it from the *vaporetto* 1, which takes you from San Lucia station to Piazza San Marco, departing every 10 minutes (every hour from 1 to 4am, €5). You really shouldn't miss a gondola ride along the quieter canals, either.

FINDING YOUR WAY

Next to each address in the Where to stay, Shopping and Going Out sections, we have given details of the nearest *vaporetti* stop in parenthesis.

cultural events, the festivals, the concerts day by day: www.culturaspettacolovenezia.it and www.veneziacultura.it. See also pp. 20-21.

How to make reservations

Apart from operas or very popular ballets for which it will be difficult to obtain a ticket without reserving several weeks in advance (try your luck all the same), it should not be difficult to secure a seat for a concert or a play.
To attend a concert in a church is sometimes even more simple: You just have to go there during the day and buy your ticket. Check the news (read above), the small posters in the streets or head to the following:
– La Fenice theater, San Marco 2549, Campo San Fantin, ☎ 041 241 80 33 (Mon.-Sat. 8.30am – 6.30pm). You can get tickets for La Fenice, of course, but also for all the other important places in Venice, theaters, churches, etc. without having to pay a commission. You can reserve and pay by phone and online on www.teatrolafenice.it, by fax at Ⓕ 041 786 580
– Vivaldi Store, San Marco, 5537/40, Campo San Bartolomeo ☎ 041 522 13 43 (Mon.-Sat. 9.30am-7.30pm, Sun. 11am-7pm). Tickets for the operas, the theaters and the concerts in churches. Commission payable.
– A travel agent. List in *Un ospite di Venezia*. Commission payable.
– The ticket office at San Marco 1810 (calle dei Fuseri), Piazzale Roma, Ferrovia Scalzi. Mon.-Sat. 8.30am-6.30pm. Call center: ☎ 041 24 24.

Prices

Prices for a concert are around €15–30, often cheaper in churches. A seat in a theater costs from €8 to €30 at the Goldoni. To attend an opera, expect to pay between €25 and €35; at La Fenice, the prices for good seats start at €60 (up to €150), a little less at the Malibran. The prices vary, of course, depending on the kind of seats (dress circle, visibility, etc.) and the fame of the guest artists. A few concerts – especially in the churches – are free (for instance some organ concerts on Saturdays at 4pm in La Salute basilica). The price of a seat in a movie theater is around €10.

La *passeggiata*

The traditional *passegiatta*, the ritual Italian stroll before dinner takes place in Venice as in the other places all year round, usually between 7pm and 8pm.

Dress code and style

Generally speaking, Venetians have a sense of style. Follow their example: Use your good sense and adapt your dress to the place you are going to spend your evening in: casual in a bar, more sophisticated in a piano bar or at the theater, and so on.

Lively spots to meet

Venetians meet on the various *campi* all of which have their regular visitors. Campo S. Luca tends to attract teenagers. Campo S. Stefano is smarter. Before going for dinner, it is the place to have a spritz, the Campari-based Venetian aperitif. Finally, Campo S. Margherita is the meeting place for students and intellectuals alike. Anyway, you will be able to go for a drink after dinner in one of the many bars in the area.

Music and theater

1 - Teatro Carlo Goldoni
2 - Teatro Malibran
3 - Church of S. M. della Pietà
4 - Rossini

Opera, theater and concerts

Foundation Cini

San Giorgio Maggiore, San Marco (S. Giorgio)

Information & reservations ☎ 041 520 55 58.

As well as major concerts, there are lectures (in Italian, of course). It's also a unique opportunity to see the Palladian cloisters around which this important foundation has grown up.

Teatro Carlo Goldoni

San Marco, 4650/B (Rialto) ☎ 041 240 20 11 Reservations at the theater Mon.-Fri. 9am-1pm and 2-4.30pm.

Probably the most interesting theater in the city. You may see the plays of Goldoni performed here, as well as contemporary repertory and even musicals. The season is from November to June.

Church of S. M. della Pietà

Riva degli Schiavoni, Castello (S. Zaccaria) ☎ 041 523 10 96 Tickets and reservations at the church.

Faithful to the memory of Vivaldi, one of Venice's major music venues stages a large number of concerts of 18th-century Venetian music, featuring Vivaldi, as well as Albinoni, Galuppi, Marcello and others. If any of the best Italian exponents of the genre are performing here – Il Giardino Armonico or Europa Galante in particular – hurry for tickets.

Teatro Malibran

Campo del Teatro, 5886/A, Cannaregio
(Rialto)
Information & reservations
☎ 041 241 80 29
or 041 241 80 33.

Built in 1677, this theater is a stone's throw from the Grand Canal on the presumed site of Marco Polo's house. It was recently restored and is dedicated to Maria Malibran (1808–1836), a singer with an amazing vocal range, who died tragically young after falling from a horse. The theater hosts concerts and operas.

Teatro Fondamente Nuove

Fondamente Nuove, 5013, Cannaregio
(Fondamente Nuove)
Information & reservations
☎ 041 522 44 98.

A theater with an interesting program, which includes world music concerts.

Teatro a l'Avogaria

Dorsoduro, 1617
(S. Basilio)
☎ 041 520 61 30.

This theater often stages productions in the Venetian language. If your Italian is good, you may recognise the local accent, with its slight lisp, neglect of double consonants and tendency to drop final vowels.

Teatro La Fenice

San Marco, 2546
Campo San Fantin
(Giglio)
☎ 041 241 80 33
www.teatrolafenice.it
Mon.-Sat. 8.30am-6.30pm; ticket office available.

Rebuilt exactly as it was and inaugurated at the end of 2003 (see p. 43) this "Second Empire" style theater, which can seat a thousand, is still reminiscent of the Visconti film *Senso* (1954), in which some scenes were shot here. It is partly thanks to him that it was possible to rebuild the

Fenice in its original colors. It is essential that opera lovers reserve seats for evening performances in the legendary Fenice, where the greatest singers in the world have performed. This is *the* place to go to see operas, concerts and ballets.

In addition...

The ballroom of the Ca' Rezzonico (www.museicivicivenezziani.it) and the numerous concerts offered in the churches and the *scuole* should set your stay in Venice to music. Don't hesitate to grant yourself this pleasure.

Movie theaters

Giorgione

Cannaregio, 4612,
(Ca' d'Oro)
☎ 041 522 62 98.

Two screens and a program which concentrates on experimental or art house film. A short distance from Strada Nuova.

Rossini

S. Marco, 3988
(Vallaresso)
☎ 041 523 03 22.

The latest movies and box office hits. You'll be able to hear Tom Hanks and Leonardo di Caprio speaking Italian behind piazza San Marco.

Videoteca Pasinetti

Palazzo Carminati, Scuola Morosini, 1882, San Stae
(S. Stae)
☎ 041 524 13 20.

The Venice video theater, where you can see fascinating movies in their original language. There are two shows a day, generally at 4pm and 9pm.

Open-air movies

In summer in Campo S. Polo (*vaporetti* 1 and 82, S. Tomà), you can see open-air movie shows every evening. During the Mostra, the movies taking part in the competition are shown

GAY VENICE

Although homosexuality is legal in Italy, gay life tends to be very discreet in the Serenissima. There are not really any gay or gay-friendly places in Venice. Mestre and Padua tend to be more open to gay culture and nightlife.

the day after the official performance for those who were unable to be present. The programs appear in the daily newspapers *Il Gazzettino* and *Nuova Venezia*, as well as in the monthly *Un Ospite di Venezia*.

Addresses in the Mostra

Palazzo del Cinema

Lungomare Marconi, Lido (Lido); ☎ 041 272 65 01.

Astra

Via Corfù, 9, Lido (Lido)
☎ 041 526 02 89.

Piano bars, jazz bars and late-night bars

Al Paradiso perduto

Fondamenta della Misericordia, 2540, Cannaregio
(S. Marcuola – B1-2)
☎ 041 72 05 81
Every day except Tue. and Wed. 7pm-2am (Sun. 12pm-2am).

An authentic *osteria* where you can dine to the sound of jazz. There's live music on Sunday and Monday, and poetry readings on Monday as well. Warm atmosphere. A unique Venetian experience – don't miss it!

Devil's Forest

Campo San Bartolomeo, Rialto, San Marco
(Rialto)
☎ 041 520 06 23
Every day 10am-midnight.

A nice, friendly pub a few minutes from the Rialto, offering a good choice of draft beers and sandwiches if you're feeling hungry at the end of the evening. You can play darts and backgammon here. Take the alley to the right of the Disney Store.

Caffè dei Frari

Fondamenta dei Frari, 2564, San Polo (S. Tomà)

☎ 041 524 18 77
Every day except Sun. 8am-9pm.

A warm wood-paneled café on two floors with a mezzanine, next to the grandiose church of the Frari. Lots of young people and a pleasant atmosphere.

Le Bistrot de Venise

Calle dei Fabbri, 4685, S. Marco
(Vallaresso or Rialto)
☎ 041 523 66 51
www.bistrotdevenise.com
Every day 9.30am-1.30am.

Don't hesitate to visit this bistrot where you can have a late dinner to musical accompaniment and enjoy cabaret acts and other live performances. The Bistrot de Venise is also a meeting place for Venetian artists. There are regular poetry readings. Traditional Venetian cooking and an excellent wine list.

Bacaro Jazz

San Marco, 5546
(Vallaresso)
☎ 041 528 52 49
Every day except Wed. 4pm-3am.

The Bacaro Jazz Venezia is located just in front of the central

SELECT BARS

These bars have a particularly elegant Venetian atmosphere.
– Lovers of design will like the lounge of the Monaco e Grand Canal (San Marco 1332, calle Vallaresso, ☎ 041 520 02 11) which, as its name indicates, overlooks the canal. Closes around 1am.
– The Dandolo bar, in the historic Hotel Danieli (Castello 4196, riva degli Schiavoni, ☎ 041 522 64 80). 9.30am-1.30am.
– The Longhi bar in the Gritti Palace (San Marco 2467, Campo Santa Maria del Giglio, ☎ 041 794 611). Like the Danieli, the Gritti has seen all the writers, aristocrats, poets and celebrities – or at least most of them. Closes around midnight.
– And the unmissable if somewhat chic Florian (Piazza San Marco 56-59, ☎ 041 520 56 41). 10am-midnight. Closed Wed. in winter.
– A short distance from La Fenice, the Centrale is an exciting restaurant lounge (San Marco 1659/B, piscina Frezzeria, ☎ 041 296 06 64). Decorated in red, pink and black 7pm-2am.

1 - Le Bistrot de Venise
2 - Devil's Forest
3 - Al Paradiso perduto

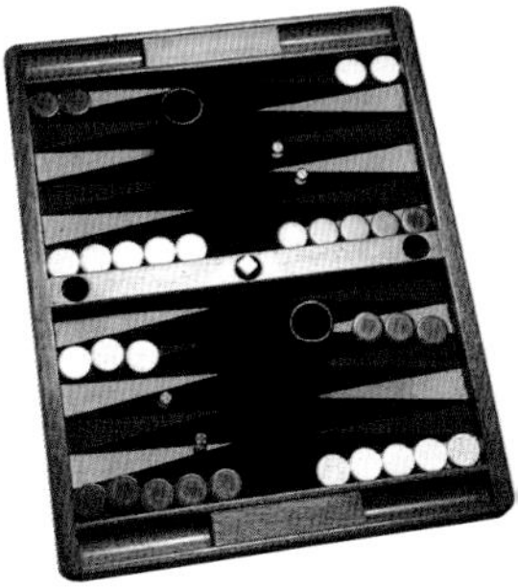

2

3

post office. If you're in the area, don't hesitate to walk into this restaurant and wine bar, whose atmosphere is very friendly and where you can listen to live music.

Imagina

Rio terrà Canal, 3126, Dorsoduro (Ca' Rezzonico)
☎ 041 241 06 25
Every day 10am-2am.

You can drink, eat and talk here. One of the rare places frequented by artists and fashion seekers. Exhibits of artists' works on the walls. Between the Santa Margherita and Santa Barnaba *campi*.

Tappa Obbligatoria

Strada Nova, 4000, Cannaregio (Ca' d'Oro)
☎ 041 520 06 68
Every day 7am-1am; closed Sun. in winter.

Enjoy *spritz*, beer, a cocktail or *ombra* as an aperitif in this place with its modern design where you can have dinner late at night. International food. Nothing extravagant but a lively place to stop at in this district which goes to sleep when the many stores of the Strada Nova have closed.

Martini Scala

Campo S. Fantin, 1983, S. Marco (Giglio)
☎ 041 522 41 21
Every day except Tue. 10pm-3.30am; Closed Jul.-Aug.

The piano bar of the Antico Martini restaurant, where you can go for a drink in elegant company.

Iguana Café

Fondamenta della Misericordia, 2515, Cannaregio (San Marcuola)
☎ 041 71 35 61
Every day 6pm-1am; closed Mon.

If the Paradiso Perduto is overcrowded, go and have a *mescal* or a *margarita* in this Mexican restaurant. Happy hour until 8pm. Concert at 9pm.

Ai Postali

Fondamenta rio Marin, 821, Santa Croce (Riva di Biasio or Ferrovia)
☎ 041 71 51 56
Every day except Sun. 6pm-2am.

A lively young bar off the beaten tourist

Cap Horn

Calle San Pantalon, 3740, Dorsoduro
(S. Tomà)
☎ 041 524 21 77
Every day 10.30am-2pm; closed Sun. in summer.

You can have a drink while listening to music, have a snack – ask for their delicious *tartinesi* – and with a little luck there might even be a live band playing.

L'Olandese volante

Campo S. Lio, 5658, Castello
(Rialto)
☎ 041 528 93 49
Mon.-Thu. 11am-12.30am, Fri.-Sat. 11am-2am, Sun. 4.30pm-12.30am.

A pleasant pub with a good location in Campo S. Lio. Wide choice of beers and sandwiches.

The Fiddler's Elbow Irish Pub

Corte dei Pali, 3847, Cannaregio (Ca' d'Oro)
☎ 041 523 99 30
Every day except Wed. (in winter) 5pm-12.30am.

An Irish pub frequented by a mixture of tourists and young Venetians. Good choice of draft and bottled beers and excellent Irish coffee. Pleasant atmosphere with concerts some evenings.

THE CHARM OF THE *CALLE* BY NIGHT

Feel like taking a night-time stroll in the Serenissima? Then go ahead – it's when Venice takes on a truly fantastic face. In some districts, you'll be able to walk for hours without meeting a living soul apart from the cats. The walk in the north of Cannaregio, from the Church of the Madonna dell'Orto to the Ghetto, will leave you with a fond memory. So, too, will a wander through the *calle* of the Castello district, from S. Zaccaria to the Arsenal. San Polo and Dorsoduro, on the other side of the Grand Canal, are fascinating when the city of the Doges sleeps. Starting in Campo S. Polo, go and see the illuminated Church of the Frari, then make your way to Campo S. Pantalon through the dark streets before returning to the lively atmosphere of Campo S. Margherita, where the bars stay open late.

In addition...

See pp. 94–95 "*Bacari* and wine bars" section: Some are open very late. Read also *Il Gazettino* or *Venezia da vivere* (see pp. 128–129) for live music in bars and nightclubs in Mestre or the Lido.

Discos

Round Midnight

Fondamenta dello Squero, 3102, Dorsoduro
(Ca' Rezzonico)
☎ 041 523 20 56
Thu.-Sat. midnight-4am.

A tiny place with a New York atmosphere a stone's throw from Campo Santa Margherita. You can listen to high-quality music (acid jazz and trip hop) here, as well as dancing the tango or watching a cabaret show. You'll find guides to the shows (*Venezia da Vivere*) in the cafés in the *campo*.

1 - *Round Midnight*
2 - *Casino di Venezia*
3 - *L'Olandese volante*

Discobar Acropolis

Lungomare Marconi, 22, Lido (Lido)
☎ 041 526 04 66
In season, Wed.-Sun. 11pm-4am; in winter only Sat.

The Lido discobar overlooks the sea. You can come for an after-dinner drink, to dance or to be seen during the Mostra del Cinema. The nightclub also has a terrace and a bar which are open between 10pm and 2am in season. They play different music every night.

Casanova

Lista di Spagna, 158/A, Cannaregio (Ferrovia)
☎ 041 275 01 99
Every day except Sun.-Tue. 6pm-4am.

The Venice discobar is right by the station, so it's very handy even if you're staying on the mainland. Its decor is an avant-garde version of the old Venetian palaces. Entry is free and happy hour goes on until 10pm, which is rare in Venice.

Casinos

Palazzo del Casino

Lungomare Marconi, 4, Lido (Lido); ☎ 041 529 71 11
Every day from 4pm; from 11am for the machines below.

Next to the Palazzo del Cinema (where movies are shown during the Mostra festival) and to the neo-Moorish Grand Hotel Excelsior. It's a chance to experience all kinds of thrills (roulette, blackjack, slot machines, etc.), and to see the luxurious Hôtel des Bains, which was immortalized by Visconti in *Death in Venice*.

Casino di Venezia

Ca' Vendramin-Calergi
Calle larga Vendramin, Cannaregio (S. Marcuola)
☎ 041 529 71 11
From 3pm.

The Venice Casino has its winter quarters on the banks of the Grand Canal, in this superb Renaissance palace dating from the early 16th century, where Richard Wagner died in 1883. It makes a choice setting in which to make a dent in your pocket playing roulette, blackjack or other less ruinous games, the slot machines in particular. For a real treat, arrive in a gondola.

Metric Conversion Chart

Note that in Italy "size" has two different translations. For clothes *la taglia* is size; for shoes, size is *il numero*.

Women's sizes

Shirts/dresses

U.K.	U.S.A.	EUROPE
8	6	36
10	8	38
12	10	40
14	12	42
16	14	44
18	16	46

Sweaters

U.K.	U.S.A.	EUROPE
8	6	44
10	8	46
12	10	48
14	12	50
16	14	52

Shoes

U.K.	U.S.A.	EUROPE
3	5	36
4	6	37
5	7	38
6	8	39
7	9	40
8	10	41

Men's sizes

Shirts

U.K.	U.S.A.	EUROPE
14	14	36
14½	14½	37
15	15	38
15½	15½	39
16	16	41
16½	16½	42
17	17	43
17½	17½	44
18	18	46

Suits

U.K.	U.S.A.	EUROPE
36	36	46
38	38	48
40	40	50
42	42	52
44	44	54
46	46	56

Shoes

U.K.	U.S.A.	EUROPE
6	8	39
7	9	40
8	10	41
9	10.5	42
10	11	43
11	12	44
12	13	45

More useful conversions

1 centimeter	0.39 inches	1 inch	2.54 centimeters
1 meter	1.09 yards	1 yard	0.91 meters
1 kilometer	0.62 miles	1 mile	1. 61 kilometers
1 liter	2.12 (US) pints	1 (US) pint	0.47 liters
1 gram	0.035 ounces	1 ounce	28.35 grams
1 kilogram	2.2 pounds	1 pound	0.45 kilograms

Published by AA Travel Publishing.

First published as Un grand week-end à Venise: © Hachette Livre (Hachette Tourisme), 2005
Written by Denis Montagnon, Antonia Naïm and Gaëlle Redon
Maps within the book © Hachette Tourisme

Published by AA Publishing, a trading name of Automobile Association Developments Limited, whose registered office is Fanum House, Basing View, Basingstoke, Hampshire RG21 4EA. Registered number 1878835.

ISBN-10: 0-7495-4843-6
ISBN-13: 978-0-7495-4843-8

Original English translation by Margaret Rocques and Anthony Moinet © Hachette Livre (Hachette Tourisme), 2005
Additional translation work by G and W Advertising and Publishing © Automobile Association Developments Limited 2006

Cover design by Bookwork Creative Associates, Hampshire
Cover maps produced from map data © New Holland Publishing (South Africa) (Pty) Ltd, 2005

Colour separation by Kingsclere Design and Print
Printed and bound in China by Leo Paper Products

Cover credits
Front cover : AA World Travel Library/Clive Sawyer; **Back cover** : Robert Lesile (top), Nicolas Edwige (bottom)

Picture credits
Nicolas Edwige: pp. 2, 3, 4, 12 (b.), 13 (c., b.), 16 (b. r.), 17 (c.), 18, 19 (t), 20 (t r.), 22 (t r., b.), 30 (t l.), 31 (b.), 32 (b.), 33 (t), 34, 38, 39, 41 (c. l.), 42 (b. r.), 43 (t c., t r., b.), 45 (t r.), 50, 53, 54 (b. l.), 57 (t, c.), 58, 59 (t), 60, 61 (c., b.), 63 (c. r.), 65 (t l.), 67 (t, c. c.), 72, 73, 74, 75 (c. l.),
76 (t r.), 77, 78, 79, 80, 81, 82, 83, 84, 86, 87, 88, 89, 90, 91, 92, 93, 94, 95 (b.), 96, 97 (t, c. r.), 98 (t l.), 99 (b. l.), 100, 102 (t r., b.), 103, 104 (t l., t r.), 105 (c.), 106 (t l., t r.), 107, 108 (t r.), 109 (t), 110, 111 (c.), 112 (b.), 113 (t c., c. r.), 114 (t l., t r.), 115 (t), 116 (t l., b.), 117, 118 (b.), 120 (t l., t r.), 124 (b. l.), 126 (t r.), 127 (c.), 128, 130 (t r., c. l., c. r.), 131, 132, 133 (t r., b. c.), 134, 135 (t l., t r.).
R. Leslie: pp. 10 (b.), 12 (t l.), 13 (t), 14 (t l.), 16 (t l., b. l.), 19 (t l., b.), 21 (b.), 24 (t l.), 26 (t l.), 28, 29, 31 (t), 32 (t l., t r.), 33 (b.), 43 (t l.), 45 (c. l.), 47 (b.), 48 (c. r.), 49 (t, b.), 51 (t), 52, 56, 62, 63 (c. l., b. l.), 65 (t c., b.), 66, 67 (c. r.), 70 (b. r.), 71 (t r., b.), 95 (t), 97 (c. l.), 98 (t r., c. l.), 99 (c., b. r.), 104 (b.), 112 (t l.), 113 (c. l.), 115 (b. l.), 116 (t r.), 118 (t r.), 120 (b.), 121 (b. l., b. r.), 122, 124 (t r., b. r.), 126 (t l.), 127 (t), 130 (t l., b.), 133 (t l., c. l.), 135 (c. c., b.).
Ch. Sarramon: pp. 10 (t r.), 11 (c.), 12 (t r.), 14 (t r., b.), 15, 16 (t r.), 17 (t), 19 (b.), 22 (t l.), 23 (c. l., b.), 24 (t l., b. l., b. r.), 25, 26 (t r., b.), 27, 30 (t r.), 40, 41 (c. r., b.), 42 (b. l.), 44, 45 (b.), 46, 47 (t l., t r., c. l.), 48 (b. l.), 49 (c.), 51 (c., b.), 54 (c. r.), 55, 57 (b.), 59 (b.), 61 (t), 63 (b. r.), 64, 68, 69, 70 (b. l.), 71 (t l.), 75 (c. r.), 76 (t l.), 98 (c. r.), 108 (t l., b.), 109 (c.), 111 (b.), 112 (t r.), 114 (b.), 115 (b. r.), 123 (c. l.), 124 (t l.), 125 (b. l.), 127 (b.).
L. Parrault: pp. 118 (t l.), 119 (c. r.), 125 (c. r.).
Hachette: pp. 11 (t r.), 11 (b.), 23 (t), 123 (t).
Taglia & Incolla: pp. 30 (b.), 126 (b. c., b. r.).
Versace: p. 102 (t. l.).
Gilberto Penzo: p. 105 (t).
Gualti: p. 106 (b.).
Madera: p. 119 (c. l.).
Gonzales: p. 121 (t).
A. Barutti: p. 125 (b. r.).
Droits réservés: pp. 10 (t l.), 21 (t).

Illustrations
Pascal Garnier

A02680